THE LIFE OF ABRAHAM

THE OBEDIENCE
OF FAITH

THE
LIFE
OF
ABRAHAM

F.B. MEYER

Edited for Today's Reader by
LANCE WUBBELS

Emerald
Books

P.O. Box 635
Lynnwood, Washington 98046

Scripture quotations are taken from the King James Version of the Bible.

The Life of Abraham

ISBN 1-883002-34-6
Published by Emerald Books
P.O. Box 635
Lynnwood, Washington 98046

Printed in the United States of America.

PREFACE

*I*n attempting to write these studies in the life of
Abraham, I am very aware of the inadequacy of my endeavor to
conceive or portray one of the greatest characters of history. And yet
there is one thought pervading the entire narrative that brings it
near to the poorest illuminator of its noble outlines. Abraham was
great through his faith. And that faith was at first but a silver thread,
a tiny streak, an insignificant straw—not stronger than that which
trembles in the humblest and weakest reader of these lines.

But wherever faith is, it is the link with omnipotence. It is the
channel for the divine communications, the wire along which the
fire of heaven may travel. And as faith is used according to the
promptings of the divine Spirit and in obedience to His commands,
it will grow. It grew in Abraham. It will grow in us.

These pages have been written to trace the laws of the growth
of Abraham's faith for the encouragement of those who by faith are
the children of Abraham and who long with intense desire to imitate their great forefather until they can remove mountains of
difficulty and achieve apparent impossibilities in and through their
lives.

F.B. Meyer

ABOUT THE EDITOR

LANCE WUBBELS, the Managing Editor of Bethany House Publishers, taught biblical studies courses at Bethany College of Missions for many years. He is also the author of *The Gentle Hills* fiction series and a heartwarming short novel, *One Small Miracle*, with Bethany House.

As the compiler and editor of the Charles Spurgeon and F.B. Meyer Christian Living Classic books, Wubbels' desire is to present these classic writings in a way that will appeal to a wide audience of readers and allow their timeless messages to be as relevant today as the day they were penned. The writings of both Spurgeon and Meyer are filled with practical insight that will enrich believers' lives.

CONTENTS

INTRODUCTION

For over a century, the writings of F.B. Meyer have provided Christians with a treasure trove of lasting value, affirming the truths of the gospel for every age. Crowning a life of worldwide ministry by voice and pen, Meyer's books reflect a depth of spiritual experience and singlemindedness of vision that one rarely finds in contemporary writing. It is for this reason that Lance Wubbels has chosen to edit and update this remarkable biography of one of God's greatest biblical saints.

F.B. Meyer wrote twelve portraits of the giants of the Old and New Testaments. These detailed, inspirational biographies are filled with insight, challenge, and comfort. It is comforting to find that these great figures were not so different from ourselves—sometimes weak, indifferent, willful. Yet they had their moments of faith, humility, and courage, and God was able to use these for His greater purposes. God's faithfulness, which not only accepts but transforms such inconsistency, calls us to more effective Christian living.

It cannot be stressed enough that these are thoroughly biblical portraits. It is essential to keep in mind that Meyer wrote every chapter with it firmly in his thoughts that the reader would have his Bible opened to the scripture at the beginning of the chapter and be completely familiar with its context. Attempting to read the chapter without studying the scripture will leave the reader in the dark at some points. The editor gives his strongest recommendation that you first read the scripture and then follow along as Meyer develops his thoughts based upon the biblical text.

You are invited to read these powerful chapters as you would listen to a trusted and skilled pastor. There is nothing speculative about Meyer's teaching. He will meet you where you live in an understandable manner that inspires and challenges, and you will not be disappointed. Life-changing messages await your reading.

Careful editing has helped to sharpen the focus of these messages and update the language while retaining the authentic and timeless flavor they undoubtedly bring.

1

THE HOLE
OF THE PIT

The God of glory appeared unto our father Abraham,
when he was in Mesopotamia, before he dwelt in Charran,
and said unto him, Get thee out of thy country, and from thy kindred,
and come into the land which I shall shew thee.

Acts 7:2–3

Look unto the rock whence ye are hewn,
and to the hole of the pit whence ye are digged.
Look unto Abraham your father.

Isaiah 51:1–2

*I*n the gray dawn of history the first great biblical character that captures our attention is Abraham. Abraham commands our notice for this reason, if for nothing else, that he is spoken of as the "friend of God." Surely it is well worth our serious consideration to study the inner life and outward conduct of such a man of God. From his life we discover that we, too, in our smaller measure may become not God's servants only but God's "friends" and favored confidants, from whom He will not hide His secrets and to whom He will make known His will.

Many rays of interest come into focus in the story of Abraham, whose portrait is drawn with such detail that it lives before us with the same hopes and fears, golden hours and hours of depression, that are familiar factors in our own lives. Then, also, Abraham is so constantly referred to in both the Old and the New Testaments that it would seem as if the right understanding of his life is necessary to give us the clue to many difficult biblical passages and many sacred doctrines of our faith. Nor can it fail to interest us to discover the reason why the wild Bedouin of the desert and the modern Englishman, the conservative East and the progressive, swift-moving West, the Muslim and the Christian can find in the tent of the first Hebrew a common meeting ground, and in Abraham a common origin.

Our story takes us back two thousand years before the birth of Christ to the ancient city of Ur. It is helpful, by the aid of modern archeological discoveries, to consider the earliest conditions around which this life was cradled. We like to stand in that lone spot among the hills where, from some moss-grown basin of rock, there springs forth the river that drains a continent and flows bearing the great ships to the sea. We ask the biographer to tell us something of the scenes amid which a great life was nurtured, because we think that we can better understand its brilliance, progression, and direction. So we can thank modern discoveries for having cast a lantern on the ruins of that old world city, which was the busy home of life when flocks browsed on the seven hills of Rome and red deer, light of foot, roamed over the site of St. Paul's Cathedral or came down to drink the undefiled and clear waters of the Thames River.

We must look for Ur, not in Upper Mesopotamia, where a mistaken tradition had fixed it, but in the ruins of Mugheir, in the near vicinity of the Persian Gulf. Forty centuries of silt building up on the shore have driven the Persian Gulf back about a hundred miles. But at the time of Abraham, it is probable that the city of Ur stood upon the coast near the spot where the Euphrates poured the volume of its waters into the ocean waves.

Professor Rawlinson has said that "the present remains of the town consist of a series of low mounds disposed in an oval shape, measuring about two miles in extent, and commanded by a larger mound of seventy feet in height, on which are the remains of what must have been once a vast temple, dedicated to the Moon." In ancient days, it was a large and flourishing city, standing on the sea and possessed of fleets of vessels that coasted along the shores of the Indian Ocean, freighted with the products of the rich and fertile soil.

It is beyond my purpose to attempt a description of the luxuriance of that Chaldean land, watered by its two mighty streams, the

Euphrates and the Tigris, and in which the corn crop was of marvelous abundance and the date palm attained to an extraordinary growth, repaying richly the scanty labors of the people, and where pomegranates and apples, grapes and tamarisks grew wild. Suffice it to say that it was a long green strip of garden land, sufficient to attract and maintain vast populations, and especially suitable for the settlement of those shepherd tribes that required extensive pasturelands for their herds and flocks.

The descendants of Ham who populated this land were grossly *idolatrous*. In its crystal clear skies, the heavenly bodies blazed with extraordinary radiance, beguiling the early Chaldeans into a system of nature worship, which soon became identified with ceremonies of gross indulgence and impurity, such as those into which humanity always falls when it refuses to retain God in its knowledge and gives itself up to the dictates of its own carnal lusts (Rom. 1:23–25). The human race seemed verging again on the brink of those horrible and unnatural crimes that had already necessitated its almost total destruction in the days of Noah, and it was evident that some means must be quickly adopted to stop the progress of moral defilement and to save mankind. This enterprise was undertaken by God Himself, whose delights have ever been with the sons of men and who, in later days, could say, with majestic emphasis, "Before Abraham was, I am" (John 8:58). And God accomplished His purpose then, as He has so often since, by *separating* to Himself one man, that through that man and his descendants, when they had been thoroughly purified and prepared, He might work upon the fallen race of man, recalling it to Himself and elevating it by a moral lever, working on a pivot outside itself.

Four centuries had passed away since the flood of Noah, and they must have been centuries abounding in emigration. Population multiplied more rapidly than now, and all the world was open before them to choose. Leaving the first localities of life, swarm after swarm of peoples must have hived off in every direction. Surging waves of men, pressed on by hunger, love of conquest, or stronger hordes behind, spread outward over the world. The sons of Japheth pushed northward to colonize Europe and Asia and to lay the foundations of the great Indo-European family. Sons of Ham pushed southward over the fertile plains of Chaldea, where, under the lead of the mighty Nimrod, they built towns of baked clay, erected temples, of which the ruins remain to this day, and cultivated the arts of civilized life to an extent unknown elsewhere. They are said to have been proficient in mathematics and astronomy, to have been skilled in weaving, metal working, and gem engraving, and to have preserved their thoughts by writing on clay tablets.

Now it happened that into the midst of this Hamite colonization there had come a family of the sons of Shem. This clan, under the lead of Terah, had settled down on the rich pasturelands outside Ur. The walled cities, civilized arts, and merchant traffic had little attraction for them because they were a race of shepherds, living in tents or in villages of slightly constructed huts. And if Noah's prediction was verified (Gen. 9:26), we may believe that their religious life was sweeter and purer than that of the people among whom we find them.

But, alas, the moral virus soon began its work. The close association of this Shemite family with the idolatrous and abominable practices of the children of Ham tainted the purity and simplicity of its early faith. It is certain that a leveling-down process was subtly at work, lowering its standard to that of its neighbors. Joshua says distinctly that the fathers of the children of Israel, who dwelt beyond the flood of the Euphrates, served other gods (Josh. 24:15). And there are traces of the evil in the home of Laban from which Rachel stole the images (*teraphim*), the loss of which so kindled her father's wrath (Gen. 31:19–35). It is a heavy responsibility for godly people to live in the midst of notorious godlessness and sin. If they escape the snare, their children may be caught in it. What right have we to heedlessly expose young lives to noxious moral vapors that may taint and defile them forever! And if through the claims of duty we are compelled to live in any such deadly and dangerous atmosphere, let us ask that the fire of divine purity may extend like a chain of defense around our home and that our dear ones may dwell in the secret place of the Most High.

Amid such scenes, Abraham was born and grew from youth to manhood. But from the first, if we can believe the traditions that have lingered in the common talk of the unchanging East, Abraham must have possessed no ordinary character. According to these stories, which, if not literally true, are no doubt based on a substratum of fact, as a young man, Abraham offered an uncompromising opposition to the evil practices that were prevalent not only in the land but also in his father's house. He employed the weapon of sarcasm that was also used so effectively afterward by the Old Testament prophets to his own descendants. He broke the helpless images to pieces. He refused to bow before the subtle element of fire at the bidding of the monarch, even under the penalty of martyrdom. Thus, early was he being detached from the quarry of heathendom, dug from "the hole of the pit," preparatory to being shaped as a pillar in the house of the Lord.

There is nothing in Scripture that describes these stories, but there is nothing inconsistent with them. On the contrary, as the peculiar movements of a planet suggest the presence of some celestial body of a definite size that is yet hidden from view in the depths of space, so the mature character, the faith, and the ready obedience of Abraham, when he first comes under our notice, convince us that there must have been a long previous period of severe trial and testing. The mushroom is the child of a single night; but the oak, which is a match for the violent storm, is the result of long years of sun and air, of breeze and storm.

At last, the God of glory appeared to Abraham. The light had been growing on his vision, and finally the sun broke out from the obscuring clouds. In what form of glory Jehovah revealed Himself we cannot guess, but we must believe that there was some outward manifestation that dated an epoch in Abraham's life, giving him an unmistakable basis of belief for all his future. Probably the Son of God, who from all eternity has been the Word of God, arrayed Himself, as He did afterward on the plains of Mamre, in an angel's form, or spoke to him, as He did afterward to Isaiah, from the midst of the burning seraphim (Isa. 6). In any case, the celestial vision was accompanied by a call, like that which in all ages of the world has come to loyal hearts, summoning them to awake to their true destiny and take their place in the regeneration of the world. "Get thee out of thy country, and from thy kindred, and from thy father's house, unto the land that I will shew thee" (Gen. 12:1). If we live up to our light, we shall have more light. If we are faithful in a very little, we may have the opportunity of being faithful in much. If we are steadfast in Chaldea, we may be called out to play a great part in the history of the world. God's choice is never arbitrary but is based on some previous traits in those whom He summons from among their fellows to His service. "For whom he did foreknow, he also did predestinate" (Rom. 8:29).

It is impossible to tell into whose hands these words may fall. Young men or women who live in the midst of the godless masses of India or in the wild bush-life of Australia. Sailors on shipboard and soldiers in camp. Lonely confessors of Christ in worldly and vicious societies, where there is everything to weaken and nothing to reinforce the resistance of the brave but faltering spirit. Let all such take heart! They are treading a well-worn path on which the noblest of mankind have preceded them. Think of how much more difficult it was in days past when few were found on it and, especially in that day, when a solitary man, the "father of many nations," trod it.

One symptom of being on that path is *loneliness*. "I called him alone" (Isa. 51:2). It was a loneliness that pressed hard on the heart of Jesus. But it is a loneliness that is assured of the divine companionship (John 8:16, 29; 16:32). And though no eye seems to notice the struggles, protests, and endeavors of the solitary spirit, they are watched with the sympathy of all heaven. Soon there will be heard a call, like the call that started Abraham as a pilgrim and opened before him the way into marvelous blessedness.

Despair not for the future of the world. Out of its heart will yet come those who shall lift it up to a new level. Sauls are being trained in the bosom of the Sanhedrin, Luthers in the cloisters of a church in dire need of reformation, Abrahams under the shadows of great heathen temples. God knows where to find them. And when the times are darkest, they shall lead forth a host of pilgrim spirits, numberless as the sand on the seashore or as the stardust lying thick through the illimitable expanse of space.

2

THE DIVINE SUMMONS

Get thee out of thy country, and from thy kindred,
and from thy father's house, unto a land that I will shew thee:
And I will make of thee a great nation, and I will bless thee,
and make thy name great; and thou shalt be a blessing.

Genesis 12:1–2

*W*hile Abraham was living quietly in Ur, testifying against the idolatry of his times, with all its attendant evils, and according to tradition, suffering bitter persecution for conscience' sake, "The God of glory appeared unto our father Abraham,...and said unto him, Get thee out of thy country, and from thy kindred, and come into the land which I shall shew thee" (Acts 7:2–3). This was the first of those marvelous appearances that anticipated the incarnation of Christ and marked the successive stages of God's manifestation of Himself to men.

When this divine appearance came, we do not know. It may have been in the still and solemn night or in the evening hour of meditation or amid the duties of his daily routine. But suddenly there shone from heaven a great light round about Abraham, and a visible form appeared in the heart of the glory, and a voice spoke the message of heaven in his ear. God does not appear to us in this manner now, and yet it is certain that He still speaks in the silence of the waiting spirit, impressing His will, and saying, "Get thee out." Listen for that voice in the inner shrine of your heart.

This same voice has often spoken since. It called Elijah from Thisbe, and Amos from Tekoa; Peter from his fishing nets, and Matthew from his tax booth; Cromwell from his farm in Huntingdon, and Luther from his cloister at Erfurt. It always sounds the perpetual summons of God: "Wherefore come out from among them, and be ye separate, saith the Lord, and touch not the unclean thing" (2 Cor. 6:17). Has it not come to you? Strange, if it has not. Yet, if it has, let nothing hinder your obedience. Take down your tents and follow where the God of glory beckons. In that word *come*, understand that He is moving on in front and that if you would have His companionship, you must follow.

THIS CALL INVOLVED HARDSHIP

Abraham was a childless man. He had more than enough material goods for the supply of his needs. He was deeply attached to those who were united to him by the close ties of a common nature. It was no small matter for him to break up his camp, to tear himself from his nearest and dearest, and to start for a land which, as yet, he did not know.

And so it remains. The summons of God always involves a separation from much that our natures hold dear. We must be prepared to take up our cross daily if we would follow where He points the way. Each step of real advance in the divine life will involve an altar on which some dear fragment of the self-life has been offered or a memorial stone beneath which some cherished idol has been buried.

It is true that the blessedness that awaits us will more than compensate us for the sacrifices that we may have to make. And the prospect of the future may well charm us forward; but still, when it comes to this point, there is certain to be anguish as the last link is broken, the last farewell said, and the last look taken of the receding home of past happy years. This is God's winnowing fan that clearly separates chaff and wheat. Many cannot endure a test so severe and searching in its demands. Like Pliable in *Pilgrim's*

16

Progress, they get out of the swamp by the side nearest to their home. Like the rich young ruler, they go away sorrowful from the One to whom they had come with such haste (Luke 18:18–23). Shall this be the case with you? Will you hear the call of God and shrink back from its cost? Count the cost clearly indeed; but having done so, go forward in the name and by the strength of Him in whom all things are possible and easy and safe. And in doing so, you will confirm yourself as worthy to stand with Christ in the regeneration.

Nothing is clearer today than that God is summoning the whole Church to a great advance, not only in knowledge and in spiritual experience but also in the evangelization of the world. Blessed are they who are privileged to have a share in this sublime campaign!

BUT THIS CALL WAS EMINENTLY WISE

It was wise for *Abraham himself*. Nothing strengthens us so much as isolation and uprooting. Let a young man leave his country or be put into a responsible position or be forced to his own resources, and he will develop powers of which there would have been no trace if he had always lived at home—dependent on others and surrounded by luxury. Under the wholesome demand, his soul will put forth all her native strength.

But what is true of the natural qualities of the soul is preeminently true of faith. So long as we are quietly at rest amid favorable and undisturbed surroundings, faith sleeps as an undeveloped muscle within us—a thread, a germ, an idea. But when we are pushed out from all these surroundings, with no one but God to look to, faith grows suddenly into a steel cable, a monarch oak, a master principle of the life.

As long as the bird lingers by the nest, it will never know the luxury of fight. As long as the trembling boy stays near the shoreline and toes the surf, he will not learn the ecstasy of battling with the ocean wave. As long as men cling to the material world, they cannot appreciate the reality of the promises of God. Abram could never have become Abraham, the father of the faithful, the mighty example of faith, if he had always lived in Ur. No, he must leave his happy home and journey forth into the untried and unknown, that faith may rise up to all its glorious proportions in his soul.

It may not be necessary for us to physically move away from

home and friends, but we shall have to withdraw our heart's deepest dependence from all earthly props and supports if we ever hope to learn what it means to trust simply and absolutely on the eternal God. Even at this moment, it may be that He is breaking away the shores on which we have been leaning, that the ship may glide down upon the ocean wave.

It was wise *for the world's sake.* On this one man rested the hope for the future of the world. Had he remained in Ur, it is impossible to know whether he would have continued true to God or whether he might not have been seriously infected by the idolatry around him. Or, even if Abraham had been enabled to resist the adverse influences, his family and, above all, his children might have failed beneath the terrible ordeal. Was it not, therefore, wise for the world's sake, and for the sake of the divine purposes, that he should be taken away from his home and early associations to find a fresh spiritual beginning for the human race on new soil and under new conditions?

Was it not also true that during days of abounding vice and superstition, God led the Pilgrim Fathers to cross the seas and found a new world on the inhospitable shores of New England? Has it not been the plan of the divine government in all ages? It is impossible to change our times as long as we live beneath their spell, but when we have risen up and gone, at the call of God, outside their influence, we are able to answer them with an irresistible power. Archimedes proclaimed that he could lift the world if he could obtain, outside of the world a pivot on which to rest his lever. Do not be surprised then, if God calls you out to be a people to Himself, that by you He may work with blessed power on the great world of men.

Sometimes, indeed, He bids us stay where we are, to glorify Him there. But often He bids us leave unhallowed companionships, unbelieving associations, evil fellowships and partnerships, and at great cost to get ourselves away into the isolation of a land that He promises to reveal.

This Call Was Accompanied by Promise

God's commands are not always accompanied by reasons, but they are always accompanied by promises—expressed or understood. To give reasons would promote discussion or debate, but to give a promise shows that the reason, though hidden, is all-sufficient. We can understand the promise, though the reason might baffle and confuse us. The reason is intellectual, metaphysical, spiritual, but a promise is practical, positive, literal. As a shell encloses a kernel, so do the divine commands hide promises in their heart. If the command is to "believe on the Lord Jesus Christ," the promise is "and thou shalt be saved" (Acts 16:31). If the command is to "sell that thou hast, and give to the poor," the promise is that "thou shalt have treasure in heaven" (Matt. 19:21). If the command is to "[leave] brethren, or sisters, or father, or mother, or wife, or children, or lands," the promise is that "he shall receive an hundredfold now in this time...and in the world to come eternal life" (Mark 10:29–30). If the command is to "be ye separate," the promise is that "I will receive you, and will be a Father unto you" (2 Cor. 6:17–18). So in this case to Abraham: "Although you are childless, I will make of you a great nation. Although you are the youngest son, I will bless you and make your name great. Although you are to be torn from your own family, in you shall all the families of the earth be blessed." And each of those promises has been literally fulfilled.

It may seem that the hardships involved in the summons to exile are too great to be borne, but study well the promise that God brings with it. And as the "city which hath foundations" (Heb. 11:10) looms into view, it will dwarf the proportions of the Ur in which you have been content to spend your days, and you will rise to be gone. Sometimes, therefore, it seems easier to dwell not on the sacrifice involved but on the contents of the divine and gracious promise. Bid people take, and they will give up of themselves. Let men find in Jesus the living water, and, like the woman of Samaria, they will leave their waterpots (John 4:28). Fire the hearts of the young with all the beauty and blessedness of the service of Jesus, and they will not find it so hard to leave nets and fishing boats and friends, to forsake all and follow Him. "But when it pleased God...to reveal his Son in me...immediately I conferred not with flesh and blood" (Gal. 1:15–16).

St. Francis de Sales used to say, "When the house is on fire, men are ready to throw everything out the window; and when the heart is full of God's true love, men are sure to count all else but worthless."

This Call Teaches
the Meaning of Election

Everywhere we look, we find beings and things more magnificently endowed than others of the same kind. This is very evident in the spiritual realm. And there may at first be a jarring astonishment at the apparent inequality of the divine arrangements, until we understand that the superior endowment of a few like Abraham is intended to enable them to better help and bless the rest. "I will bless thee,...and thou shalt be a blessing."

A great thinker feels that his death is approaching. While he has made grand discoveries, he has not as yet given them to the world. He selects one of his most promising students and carefully indoctrinates the student with his system. The great thinker is very severe when it comes to inaccuracies and mistakes, and he is very careful to give line on line. Why does he take all this care? For the sake of the younger man? Not exclusively for the student's benefit, but that the student may be able to give to the world those thoughts that his dying master has confided to his care. The young disciple is blessed that he may pass the blessings on to others.

Is this not a glimpse into the intention of God in selecting Abraham and, in him, the whole family of Israel? It was not so much with a view to their personal salvation, although that was included, but that they might pass on the holy teachings and oracles with which they were entrusted. It would have been worse than useless to have given such jewels directly to mankind. To say the least, there was no language ready in which to enshrine the sacred thoughts of God. The spirit of truth required that the minds of men should be prepared to apprehend its sacred lessons. It was required that definitions and methods of expression should be first well learned by the people, who, when they had learned them, might become the teachers of mankind.

The deep question is, whether election has more to do with our ministry than with our personal salvation. It brings less of rest and peace and joy than it does of anguish, bitterness, and sorrow of heart. There is no need to envy God's elect ones. They are the exiles, the crossbearers, the martyrs among men. Having crucified the flesh, they are all the while learning God's deepest lessons, away from the ordinary pursuits of men. But they return to others with discoveries that pass all human thought and are invaluable for human life.

THIS CALL GIVES THE KEY TO ABRAHAM'S LIFE

It rang a clarion note at the very outset that continued to vibrate throughout his lifetime. The key to Abraham's life is the word *separation*. Abraham was from first to last a separated man. Separated from his fatherland and kinsfolk, separated from Lot, separated as a pilgrim and stranger from the people of the land, separated from his own methods of securing a fulfillment of the promises of God, separated from the rest of mankind by the special sorrows that brought him into closer fellowship with God than has ever been reached by man, separated to high and lofty fellowship in the thoughts and plans that God could not hide from him.

BUT IT WAS THE SEPARATION OF FAITH

There is a form of separation known among men in which the lonely soul goes away to secure uninterrupted time for devotion, spending hours upon hours in fasting and prayer and hoping to win salvation as the reward for its severities. This is not the separation to which God called Abraham, or to which we are summoned.

Abraham's separation is not like that of those who wish to be saved, but it is rather like that of those who are saved. Not toward the Cross, but from it. Not to merit anything, but, because the heart has seen the Vision of God and cannot now content itself with the things that once fascinated and entranced it, so that leaving them behind, it reaches out its hands in eager longing for eternal realities and thus is led gradually out and away from the seen to the unseen, and from temporal to the eternal.

May such a separation be ours! May we catch the divine call, dazzled by the divine promise! And as we hear of that fair land, of that glorious city, of those divine delights that await us, may we leave and relinquish those lesser and detrimental things that have held us too long, spoiling our peace and sapping our power and, striking our tents, obey our God's command, though it may lead us where we know not!

3

"He Obeyed"

By faith Abraham,
when he was called to go out
into a place which he should after
receive for an inheritance, obeyed.

Hebrews 11:8

*A*h, how much there is in those two words,
Abraham obeyed! Blessedness in heart and home and life, fulfilled
promises, and mighty opportunities of good lie along the narrow,
thorn-set path of obedience to the word and will of God. If Abraham
had permanently refused obedience to the voice that summoned
him to go forth on his long and lonely pilgrimage, he would have
sunk back into the obscurity of an unknown grave in the land of Ur,
like many an Eastern sheik before and since. So does the phospho-
rescent wave flash for a moment in the wake of the vessel slicing
her way by night through the southern seas, and then it is lost to
sight forever. But, thank God, Abraham obeyed, and in that act laid
the foundation stone of the noble structure of his life.

It may be that some will read these words who feel their lives have been a sad disappointment. Perhaps you compare your life to a young fruit tree, laden in spring with blossom but which, in the golden autumn, stands barren and alone amid the abundant fruitage of the orchard. You have not done what you expected to do. You have not fulfilled the anticipations of your friends. You have failed to achieve the early promise of your life. And may not the reason lie in this, that early in your life there rang out a command from God that summoned you to an act of self-sacrifice from which you shrank? And *that* has been your one critical mistake. Disobedience is the worm at the root of the plant, the little rot within the timber, the false step that deflects one's life-course from the King's highway into a blind alley.

Would it not be best for you to determine whether this is what you did and, if so, to hasten back to fulfill even now the long-delayed obedience? Oh, do not think that it is too late to repair the error of the past. Despite your delay, the Almighty God will not refuse that to which He once summoned you in the young, glad years that have taken their flight forever. "The LORD is merciful and gracious, slow to anger, and plenteous in mercy" (Ps. 103:8). Do not use your long delay as an argument for longer delay, but use it as a reason for immediate action. "Why tarriest thou?" (Acts 22:16)

Abraham, as the biblical account shows, at first met the call of God with a mingled and partial obedience, and then for long years neglected it entirely. But the door remained open for him to enter, and that gracious hand still beckoned him until he struck his tents and started to cross the mighty desert with all those who were under his authority. It was a partial failure that is filled with invaluable lessons for us.

AT FIRST, ABRAHAM'S OBEDIENCE WAS ONLY PARTIAL

He took Terah with him. Indeed, it is said that "Terah took Abram his son, and Lot the son of Haran his son's son, and Sarai his daughter in law, his son Abram's wife; and they went forth with them from Ur of the Chaldees" (Gen. 11:31). How Terah was persuaded to leave the land of his choice and the grave where his son Haran was laid, we cannot tell. Was Abraham his favorite son, from whom Terah could not part? Was he dissatisfied with his camping grounds? Or, had he been brought to desire an opportunity of renouncing his idols and beginning a better life in the midst of healthier surroundings? We do not know. This is clear, however, that Terah was not wholehearted nor were his motives unmixed, and his presence in the march had the disastrous effect of slowing Abraham's pace and of interposing a parenthesis of years in an obedience that at first promised so well. Days that break in radiant sunlight are not always bright throughout; mists, born of earth, ascend and veil the sky: but eventually the sun breaks out again and, for the remaining hours of daylight, shines in a sky unblemished with cloud. It was so with Abraham.

The clan marched leisurely along the valley of the Euphrates, finding abundance of pasture in its broad alluvial plains, until at last the city of Haran was reached. This is the point from which caravans for Canaan leave the Euphrates to strike off across the desert. There they halted, and there they stayed until Terah died. Was it that the old man was too weary for further journeyings? Did he like Haran too well to leave it? Did Terah's heart and flesh fail as he looked out on that far expanse of level sand, behind which the sun set in lurid glory every night? In any case, he would go no farther on the pilgrimage, and it appears that for as long as fifteen years, Abraham's obedience was on hold. During those years, there is no recording of further commands, additional promises, or hallowed communings between God and His child.

From Abraham we learn that we need to be very careful as to whom we take with us in our pilgrimage. We may make a good start in departing from our Ur, but if we take Terah with us, we shall not go far. Take care, young pilgrim of eternity, to whom you mate yourself in the bonds of marriage. Beware, man of business, lest you find your Terah in the man with whom you are entering into partnership. Let us all beware of the fatal spirit of compromise that tempts us to linger where beloved ones bid us to stay. "Do not go to extremes," they cry. "We are willing to accompany you on your pilgrimage, if you will only go as far as Haran! Why think of going farther on a fool's errand, especially when you do not know where you are to go?" Such words are hard to bear, harder far than outward opposition. Weakness and debility appeal to our feelings against our better judgment. The plains of Capua do for warriors what the arms of Rome failed to accomplish. And, bewitched by the temptations that hold out their siren attractions to us, we imitate the sailors of Ulysses and vow we will go no farther in quest of our distant goal.

"When his father was dead, he removed him into this land" (Acts 7:4). Death had to interpose to set Abraham free from the deadly fiend that held him fast. Terah must die before Abraham will resume the forsaken path. Here we may discover a solution for mysteries in God's dealings with us that have long puzzled us. Here we may come to understand why our hopes have withered, our schemes have failed, our income has dwindled, and our children have turned against us. All these things were hindering our true development of character. Out of His great mercy for our best interests, God has been compelled to take the knife in hand and set us at liberty. He loves us so much that He dares to bear the pain of inflicting pain. And thus Death opens the door to Life, and through the grave we pass into the glad world of Hope and Promise that lies upon its farther side.

> *"Glory to God, 'to God,'" he saith.*
> *Knowledge by suffering entereth,*
> *And life is perfected through death.*

ABRAHAM'S OBEDIENCE WAS MADE POSSIBLE BY FAITH

"And Abram took Sarai his wife, and Lot his brother's son, and all their substance that they had gathered, and the souls that they had gotten in Haran" (Gen. 12:5). This was no easy matter! It was bitter to leave the kinsfolk that had gathered around him. It appears that Nahor followed his old father and brother up the valley to their new settlement at Haran, and we find his family living there afterward (compare Gen. 11:29; 22:20–23; 24:10; 27:43). There was no overcrowding in those ample pastures where they were. And to crown it all, the pilgrim actually did not know his destination, yet he proposed to turn his back on the Euphrates and his face toward the great desert. Do you not suppose that Nahor would make this the one subject of his attack?

"What do you want more, my brother, that you cannot have here?"

"I want nothing but to do the will of God, wherever it may lead me."

"Look at the dangers. You cannot cross the desert or go into a new country without arousing the jealousy of some and the cravings of others. You would be no match for a troop of robbers or an army of highwaymen."

"But He who bids me go must take all the responsibility of that upon Himself. He will care for us."

"Tell me, only, where you are going, and where you propose to settle."

"That is a question I cannot answer. Indeed, you know as much about it as I do myself. But I am sure that if I take one day's march at a time, that will be made clear—and the next—and the next— until at last I am able to settle in the country that God has selected for me somewhere."

This surely was the spirit of many conversations that must have taken place on the eve of that memorable departure. And the equivalents to our words *Idiot, Fanatic,* and *Fool* would be freely passed from mouth to mouth. But Abraham would quietly answer: "God has spoken; God has promised; God will do better for me than ever He has said." At night, as he paced beneath the stars, he may have sometimes been inclined to give up in despair. But then that sure promise came back again on his memory, and he braced himself to obey. "By faith Abraham, when he was called to go out into a place which he should after receive for an inheritance, *obeyed*" (Heb. 11:8). Where he was to go, he knew not; it was enough for Abraham to know that he went with God. He leaned not so much upon the promise as upon the Promiser. He looked not on the difficulties of his situation but on the King eternal, immortal, invisible, the only wise God who had deigned to appoint his course and would certainly vindicate Himself.

And so the caravan started forth. The camels, heavily laden, attended by their drivers. The vast flocks, mingling their bleatings with their drovers' cries. The demonstrative sorrow of Eastern women, mingling with the grave farewells of the men. The forebodings in many hearts of imminent danger and prospective disaster. Sarah may even have been broken down with bitter regrets. But Abraham staggered not through unbelief. He knew whom he had believed and was persuaded that He was able to keep that which he had committed to Him against that day. He was fully persuaded that what God had promised, He was able also to perform.

Moreover, the sacred writer tells us that already some glimpses of the "city which hath foundations" (Heb. 11:10) and of the "better country, that is, an heavenly" (Heb. 11:16), had loomed upon his vision, and that fair vision had loosened his grip upon much that otherwise would have fascinated and held him.

Ah, glorious faith! This is the work of faith, and these are the amazing possibilities! Abraham was content to sail with sealed orders because of unwavering confidence in the love and wisdom of the Lord High Admiral. He was willing to rise up, leave all, and follow Christ because of the glad assurance that earth's best cannot bear comparison with heaven's least.

ABRAHAM'S OBEDIENCE WAS FINALLY VERY COMPLETE

"They went forth to go into the land of Canaan; *and into the land of Canaan they came*" (Gen. 12:5). For many days after leaving Haran, the eye would sweep a vast monotonous waste, broken by the scantiest vegetation; the camels continued to tread the soft sand beneath their spreading, spongy feet; and the flocks would find but scanty nutriment on the coarse, sparse grass.

At one point only would the travelers halt their course. In the oasis where Damascus stands today, the same stood then, furnishing a welcome resting place to weary travelers over the waste. A village near Damascus is still called by the patriarch's name. And the Jewish historian Josephus tells us that in his time, a suburb of Damascus was called "the habitation of Abraham." And there is surely a trace of Abraham's short sojourn there in the name of his favorite and most trusted servant, Eliezer of Damascus, of whom we shall read later.

But Abraham would not stay here. The luxuriance and beauty of the place were very attractive, but he could not feel that it was God's choice for him. Therefore, before long, he was again on the southern track to reach Canaan as soon as he could. Our one aim in life must ever be to follow the will of God and to walk in the ways that He has preordained for us to walk. Many a Damascus oasis, where icy waters descending from mountain ranges spread a delicious coolness through the fevered air and temper the scorching heat by abundant vegetation, tempts us to tarry. Many a Peter, well meaning but mistaken, lays his hand on us, saying, "Be it far from thee, Lord: this shall not be unto thee" (Matt. 16:22). Many a conspirator within the heart counsels a general mutiny against the lonely, desolate will. And it is well when the pilgrim of eternity refuses to slack in any particular aspect of perfect consecration and obedience to the extreme demands of God. When you set out for the land of Canaan, do not rest until you come into the land of Canaan. Anything short of complete obedience nullifies all that has been done. The Lord Jesus must have all or none, and His demands must be fulfilled as He commands. But they are not grievous, as is proven in Abraham's case.

What a glorious testimony was that which our Master uttered when He said, "The Father hath not left me alone; for I do always those things that please him" (John 8:29). Would that it might be true of each of us! Let us always give to Christ our prompt and unlimited obedience. Let us be sure that even if He bids us ride into the valley of death, it is through no blunder or mistake, but out of some sheer necessity that forbids Him to treat us otherwise and that He will satisfactorily explain before long.

4

THE FIRST OF THE PILGRIM FATHERS

Abram departed...Abram passed through...
Abram went forth...Abram removed...
Abram journeyed....
Genesis 12:4–9

He went out, not knowing whither he went.
Hebrews 11:8

*A*ll through the history of mankind there has been a little band of men, in a sacred and unbroken succession, who have confessed that they were pilgrims and strangers upon earth. As the scallop shell on the monument of the cathedral aisle indicates that he whose dust lies beneath once went on a pilgrimage beyond the seas, there are certain marks that indicate the pilgrims of the Unseen and Eternal. Sometimes they are found far from the comfortable dwellings of men, wandering in deserts and in mountains, dwelling in the dens and caves of the earth—where they have been driven by those who had no sympathy with their otherworldliness, and who hated to have so strong a light thrown on their own earthly, fleshly concerns. But very often the pilgrims of God are to be found in the marketplaces and homes of men, distinguished only by their lack of concern for fashion, their restrained and moderate appetite, their loose hold on money, their independence of the maxims and opinions and applause of the world around, and the faraway look that now and again gleams in their eyes. These are the certain evidence of affections centered, not on the transitory things of time and earth, but on those eternal realities that, lying beneath the veil of the visible, are revealed only to faith.

These are the pilgrims. For them the annoyances and trials of life are not so crushing or so difficult to bear, because such things as these cannot touch their true treasure or affect their real interest. For them, the royalties and glories, the honors and rewards, and the delights and indulgences of men have no attraction. They are children of a sublimer realm, members of a greater commonwealth, citizens of a nobler city than any upon which the sun has ever looked. Foreigners may defraud an Englishman of all his spending money, but he can well afford to lose it if all his capital is safely invested at home in the Bank of England. How can the offer of ruling a petty principality present attractions to a prince who is passing hastily through the tiny territory to assume the supreme authority of a mighty monarchy? The pilgrim has no other desire than to pass quickly over the appointed route to his home—a track well trodden through all ages—fulfilling his duties, meeting the claims, and discharging faithfully the responsibilities falling upon him, but ever remembering that here he has no continuing city and seeks one that is to come.

The immortal dreamer John Bunyan, who has told the story of the pilgrims in words that the world will never let die, gives three marks of their appearance:

First: "They were clothed with such kind of raiment as was diverse from the raiment of any that traded in that fair. The people, therefore, of the fair made a great gazing upon them; some said they were fools, some they were Bedlams; and some they were outlandish men."

Second: "Few could understand what they said, they naturally spoke the language of Canaan: but they that kept the fair were the men of this world; so that from one end of the fair to the other they seemed barbarians to each other."

Third: "But that which did not a little amuse the merchandisers was, that these pilgrims set very light by all their wares;

they cared not so much as to look upon them, and if they called on them to buy, they would put their fingers in their ears and cry, *Turn away mine eyes from beholding vanity, and look upwards*, signifying that their trade and traffic was in heaven."

Evidently this type of man was well known when that great dreamer dreamed, and long before. For the apostle Peter wrote to scattered strangers (1 Pet. 1:1) and reminded them, *as strangers and pilgrims*, to abstain from fleshly lusts. And long before that day, in the sunniest period of Jewish prosperity, David, in the name of his people, confessed that they were *strangers and sojourners as were all their fathers* and that their days on earth were as a shadow on the hills, now covering long distances of landscape, and then wasting away, chased by glints of brilliant sun (1 Chron. 29:15).

We left the patriarch Abraham moving leisurely southward; and thus he continued to journey forward through the land of promise, making no permanent halt, till he reached the place of Sichem, or Shechem, in the very heart of the land where our Lord Jesus in later years sat weary by the well. There was no city or settlement there then. The country was sparsely populated. The only thing that marked the site was a venerable oak, whose spreading arms in later ages were to shadow the excesses of a shameful idolatry (Judges 9:27–46; 1 Kings 12:25). Beneath this oak on the plain of Sichem, the camp was pitched; and there, at last, the long silence was broken that had lasted since the first summons was spoken in Chaldea: "And the LORD appeared unto Abram, and said, Unto thy seed will I give this land: and there builded he an altar unto the LORD, who appeared unto him" (Gen. 12:7).

Abraham did not, however, stay there permanently but moved a little to the south, to a place between Bethel and Ai. Here, according to Dr. Robinson, there is now a high and beautiful plain, presenting one of the finest tracts of pastureland in the whole country.

Three things, then, engage our thought: the tent, the altar, and the promise.

THE TENT

When Abraham left Haran, his age was seventy-five. When he died he was one hundred seventy-five years old. And he spent that intervening century moving to and fro, dwelling in a frail and flimsy tent, probably of dark camel's hair, like that of the Bedouin of the present day. And that tent was a fitting symbol of the spirit of his life.

Abraham held himself aloof from the people of the land. He was among them but not of them. He did not attend their tribal gatherings. He carefully guarded against intermarriage with their children, sending to his own country to obtain a bride for his son. He would not take from the Canaanites a thread or a sandal. He insisted on paying full market value for all he received. He did not stay in any permanent location but was ever on the move. The tent that had no foundations and could be set up and taken down in half an hour was the appropriate symbol of his life.

Frequently may the temptation have been presented to his mind of returning to Haran, where he could settle in the town that was identified with his family. Nor were opportunities to return lacking (Heb. 11:15). But he deliberately preferred the wandering life of Canaan to the settled home of Charran, and to the end he still dwelt in a tent. It was from a tent that he was carried to lie beside Sarah in Machpelah's rocky cave. And why? The question is fully answered in the majestic chapter that recounts the triumphs of faith. "[Abraham] sojourned in the land of promise, as in a strange country, dwelling in tabernacles with Isaac and Jacob, the heirs with him of the same promise: For he looked for a city which hath the foundations" (Heb. 11:9–10). Precisely so. The tent life is the natural one for those who feel that their homeland lies beyond the stars.

It is of the utmost importance that the children of God should live this detached life as a testimony to the world. How will people believe us when we talk about our eternal hope if we are not free from an excessive devotion to the things around us? If we are as anxious, as covetous or grasping, as dependent on the pleasures and fascinations of this passing world as unbelievers, may they not begin to question whether our profession is true and whether there is a real eternal city of God?

We must not go on as we are. Many Christians are too wrapped up in business cares, in pleasure seeking, in luxury, and in self-indulgence. There is a slight difference between the children of the kingdom and the children of this generation. The shrewdest observer could hardly detect any difference in their homes, in the education of their children, in their dress, or in their methods of doing business. They eat, they drink; they buy, they sell; they plant, they build; they marry, they give in marriage—though the flood is already breaking through the crumbling barriers to sweep them all away.

Yet how is it to be altered? Shall we denounce the present practice? Shall we protest the reckless worldliness of the times? This will not effect a permanent cure. Let us rather paint with glowing colors the eternal city that the apostle John saw by revelation. Let us unfold the glories of that matchless world to which we are bound. Let us teach that even here, the self-denying, resolute, and believing spirit may daily tread the golden pavement and hear the symphonies of angel harps. Surely there will come into many lives a separateness of heart and walk that shall impress men with the reality of the unseen, as no sermon could do, however educated or eloquent.

THE ALTAR

Wherever Abraham pitched his tent, he built an altar. Thus the Pilgrim Fathers, on the shores of New England, set up their altars of worship even before they built their homes. And long after Abraham's tent was shifted, the altar stood to show where the man of God had been.

It would be a blessed sign of our spiritual fervor if we could set up altars in every house where we pass the night and in every locality where it might be our fortune to live, setting the example of private and family prayer that would live long after we had passed away. If we would only dare to do it, the very Canaanites would come to revere the spot where we had knelt and would hand on the sacred tradition, stirring coming generations to kneel there also and call upon the name of the Lord.

Let us also remember that the altar means sacrifice, whole burnt offering, self-denial, and self-surrender. In this sense, the altar and the tent must ever go together. We cannot live the detached tent life without some amount of pain and suffering, such as the altar indicates. But it is out of such a life that the most intense devotion, the deepest fellowship, the happiest communion spring.

If your private prayer has been hindered lately, it may be that

you have not been living enough in the tent. The tent life of separation is sure to produce the altar of self-denial and of heavenly
fellowship. Confess that you are a stranger and a pilgrim on the
earth, and you will find it pleasant and natural to call on the name
of the Lord. We do not read of Abraham building an altar as long as
he dwelt in Charran. He could not have fellowship with God while
living in open disobedience to Him or as long as he was resting
comfortably in a settled life. But out of the heart of the real pilgrim
life sprang longings, desires, and aspirations that could be satisfied
only by the altars that marked his progress from place to place.

But Abraham's altar was not for himself alone. At certain
periods, Abraham's whole clan gathered there for common worship. His was a motley group in which slaves bought in Egypt or Ur
mingled together with those born in the camp, in which children
and parents, young and old, stood in silent awe around the altar,
where the patriarch stood to offer their common sacrifice and worship. "I know him," said God, "that he will command his children
and his household after him" (Gen. 18:19). Abraham, in whom all
the families of the earth were to be blessed, practiced family religion, and in this he sets a striking example to many Christians
whose homes are without an altar. Would that Christians might be
stirred by the example of the patriarch to erect the family altar and
to gather around it the daily circle of their children and dependents
for the sweetening and ennobling of their family life! Many an evil
thing, like the gargoyles on the cathedral towers, would be driven
forth before the hallowing influence of praise and prayer.

THE PROMISE

"Unto thy seed will I give this land" (Gen. 12:7). As soon as
Abraham had fully obeyed, this new promise broke upon his ear.
And it is always this way. Disobey, and you tread a path unlit by a
single star. Obey, living up to the claims of God, and successive
promises beam out from heaven to light your steps, each one richer
and fuller than the one before. Until this time, God had pledged
Himself only to show Abraham the land: now He bound Himself to
give it. The separated pilgrim life always obtains promises.

There was no natural probability of that promise being fulfilled.
"The Canaanite was then in the land" (Gen. 12:6). Powerful chieftains like Mamre and Eshcol; flourishing towns like Sodom, Salem,

and Hebron; the elements of civilization—all were there. The Canaanites were not wandering tribes. They had settled and taken root. They built towns and tilled the land. They knew the use of money and writing and administered justice in the gate. Every day built up their power and made it more unlikely that they could ever be dispossessed by the descendants of a childless shepherd.

But God had said it, and so it came to pass. "The counsel of the LORD standeth for ever, the thoughts of his heart to all generations" (Ps. 33:11). I know not what promise may be overarching your life, my reader, with its rainbow of hope; but this is certain, that if you fulfill its conditions and live up to its demands, it will be literally and gloriously fulfilled. Look not at the difficulties and improbabilities that block your path but at the might and faithfulness of the Promiser. "Heaven and earth shall pass away: but my words shall not pass away" (Mark 13:31). Not one jot or tittle shall fail (Matt. 5:18; Luke 16:17). And promise after promise shall light your life, like lighthouses at night that pass the ships onward along a rocky coast, till at last the rays of the rising sun shine full on the haven where the mariner would be.

5

GONE DOWN INTO EGYPT

Abraham went down into Egypt to sojourn there;
for the famine was grievous in the land [of Canaan].
Genesis 12:10

*T*he path of the man separated to God can never be an easy one. That man must be willing to stand alone, to go outside the camp, and to forego the aid of many of those supplies on which other men freely draw. It is a life, therefore, that is possible only to faith. When faith is strong, we dare cut ourselves adrift from the moorings that joined us to the shore, and we launch out into the deep, depending only on the character and word of Him at whose command we go. But when faith is weak, we dare not do it, and leaving the upward path, we herd with the men of the world, who have their portion in this life and who are content with that alone. Ah, how can we say enough of God's tender mercy, who, at such times, bends over us with infinite compassion, waiting to lift us back into the old heroic life!

F.B. Meyer

"And There Was a Famine in the Land"

A famine? A famine in the land of promise? Yes, as afterward, so then. The rains that usually fall in the latter part of the year had failed. The crops had been burned up with the sun's heat before the harvest. The vegetation, which should have carpeted the uplands with pasture for the flocks, was scanty or altogether absent. If a similar calamity were to befall us now, we could still draw sufficient supplies for our support from abroad. But Abraham had no such resource. A stranger in a strange land, surrounded by suspicious and hostile peoples, and carrying the responsibility of vast flocks and herds—it was no trivial matter for Abraham to stand face to face with the sudden devastation of famine.

Did the famine prove that Abraham had made a mistake in coming to Canaan? Happily, the promise that had lately come to him forbade his entertaining the thought. And this may have been one of the primary reasons why it was given. It came not only as a reward for the past but also as a preparation for the future, so that the man of God might not be tempted beyond what he was able to bear. Our Savior has His eye on our future and sees from afar the enemy that is gathering its forces to attack us or is laying its plans to beguile and entrap our feet. Jesus' heart is not more inattentive of us than, under similar circumstances, it was of Peter, in the darkening hour of his trial, when He prayed for Peter that his faith might not fail and washed his feet with an inexpressible solemnity. And thus it often happens that a time of special trial is ushered in by the shining forth of the divine presence and the declaration of some unprecedented promise. Happy are they who clothe themselves with these divine preparations and so pass unhurt through circumstances that otherwise would crush them with their inevitable pressure.

How often do some Christians adopt a hurt and injured tone in speaking of God's dealings with them? They look back upon a sunny past and complain that it was better with them before they entered by the small gate and commenced to tread the narrow way. Since that moment they have met with nothing but disaster. They had no famines in Ur or Charran; but now, in the land of promise, they are put to sore difficulties and are driven to their wits' end. The trader has met with bad debts that sorely embarrass him; the businessman has been disappointed in several of his most promising investments; the farmer has been disheartened by a succession of bad seasons. And they complain that the service of God has brought them misfortune rather than a blessing.

But this point should be borne in mind from the other side. These misfortunes would probably have come in any case, and how much less tolerable would they have been had there not been the new sweet consciousness that God had now become the refuge of the soul! Besides this, God our Father does not undertake to repay His children in the manner of this world. Spiritual grace will ever be its own reward. Purity, truth, gentleness, and devotion have no equivalent in the ore drawn from the mines of Peru or in the pearls of the sea, but only in the happy consciousness of the heart at peace with God and rejoicing in His smile. Had God pledged Himself to give His servants an unbroken run of prosperity, how many more counterfeit Christians would there be! It is good that He has made no such promise, although it is certainly true that "godliness is profitable unto all things, having promise of the life that now is, and of that which is to come" (1 Tim. 4:8). Do not be surprised if a famine meets you. It is no proof of your Father's anger but is permitted to come to test you or to root you deeper, as the whirlwind makes the tree grapple its roots deeper into the soil.

"ABRAM WENT DOWN INTO EGYPT TO SOJOURN THERE"

What a marvelous history is that of Egypt, linking successive centuries. Full of mystery, wonder, and deep thinking on the destiny of man. The land of pyramid and sphinx, of mighty dynasties, and of the glorious Nile. We need not wonder that Egypt has ever been one of the granaries of the world when we recall the periodic inundation of that marvelous river that preserves the long narrow strip of green between far-reaching wastes of sand. It is here that in all ages countries have come, as Joseph's brethren did, to buy corn. The ship in which the apostle Paul was conveyed to Rome was a corn ship of Alexandria, bearing a freight of wheat for the consumption of Rome.

In the figurative language of Scripture, Egypt stands for an alliance with the world and a dependence on an arm of flesh. "Woe to them that go down to Egypt for help; and stay on horses, and trust in chariots, because they are many; and in horsemen, because they are very strong; but they look not unto the Holy One of Israel, neither seek the LORD!" (Isa. 31:1).

There were occasions in the Jewish story when God Himself told His servants to seek a temporary asylum in Egypt. While Jacob was halting in indecision on the confines of Canaan, longing to go to Joseph and yet reluctant to repeat the mistakes of the past, Jehovah said, "I am God, the God of thy father: fear not to go down into Egypt; for I will there make of thee a great nation: I will go down with thee into Egypt" (Gen. 46:3-4). And in later days, the angel of the Lord appeared to Joseph in a dream, saying, "Arise, and take the young child and his mother, and flee into Egypt" (Matt. 2:13). There may be times in all our lives when God may clearly indicate that it is His will for us to go out into the world with a view of accomplishing some divine purpose with respect to it. "Go, shine as lights," He seems to say. "Stop the corruption, even as salt does. Witness for Me where My name is daily blasphemed." And when God sends us, by the undoubted call of His providence, He will be as sure to keep and deliver us as He did Jacob and his family, or the Holy Child.

But it does not appear that Abraham received any such divine direction. He acted simply on his own judgment. He looked at his difficulties and became paralyzed with fear. He grasped at the first means of deliverance that suggested itself, much as a drowning man will catch at a straw. And thus, without taking counsel of his heavenly Protector, Abraham went down into Egypt.

Ah, fatal mistake! But how many make it still. They may be true children of God, and yet, in a moment of panic, they will adopt methods of delivering themselves that, to say the least, are questionable, sowing the seeds of sorrow and disaster to save themselves from some minor embarrassment. Christian women plunge into the marriage bond with those who are the enemies of God so that they may be carried through some financial difficulty. Christian businessmen take ungodly partners for the sake of the capital they introduce. To enable them to fight off the pressure of difficulties and to maintain their respectability, Christian people of all grades will court the help of the world. What is all this but going down to Egypt for help?

How much better would it have been for Abraham to have thrown the responsibility back on God and to have said, "You brought me here, and You must now bear the whole weight of providing for me and my family. I will stay till I clearly know what You want me to do." If any should read these lines who have come into positions of extreme difficulty through following the simple path of obedience, let them not look at God through difficulties as we see the sun shorn of splendor through a fog. But let them look at difficulties through God as He is. Let them put God between themselves and the disasters that threaten them. Let them cast the whole responsibility upon Him. Has He not thus brought you into difficulties, that He may have an opportunity of strengthening your faith by giving some unexampled proof of His power? Wait only on the Lord, trust also in Him. His name is Jehovah-jireh; He will provide.

See How One Sin Leads to Another

When Abraham lost his faith and went down into Egypt, he also lost his courage and persuaded his wife to call herself his sister. He had heard of the licentiousness of the Egyptians and feared that they might take his life to get possession of Sarah, who, even at the age that she had reached, must have been possessed of very considerable charms.

There was an element of truth in the statement that Sarah was his half-sister. But it was meant as a lie, and it certainly misled the Egyptians, "for [she] was taken into Pharaoh's house" (Gen. 12:15). It was a mean and cowardly act on Abraham's part that was utterly indefensible. It was a cruel wrong to one who had faithfully followed his fortunes for so long. And it endangered the promised seed. Yet it continues to happen. When we lose our faith and are filled with panic for ourselves, we become unmindful of all and every tie and are prepared to sacrifice our nearest and dearest, if only we may escape.

The world may strongly appeal to us (Gen. 12:16), but that will be a poor compensation for our losses. There is no altar in Egypt, no fellowship with God, no new promises, but there is a desolated home and a wretched sense of wrong. When the prodigal leaves his father's house, though he may win a brief spell of forbidden pleasure, he loses all that makes life worth living and brings himself down to the level of the swine. In such a case, there is no recourse except to retrace the way that we have come, to "do the first works," and like Abraham to go up out of Egypt to the place of the altar where we were "at the first" (Gen. 13:4). Abraham's failure in Egypt gives us an insight into the original nature of the patriarch, which was by no means heroic and betrays a vein of duplicity and deceit similar to that which has so often reappeared in his posterity.

How thankful should we be that the Bible does not shrink from recording the story of the sins of its noblest saints! What a proof of its truthfulness is here, and what encouragement there is for us! If God was able to make His friend Abraham out of such material as this, may we not aspire to a like privilege, though we, too, have grievously violated the high calling of faith? The one thing that God requires of His saints is implicit obedience—entire surrender. Where these are present, He can still make Abrahams out of us, though, by nature, the soil of our being is prone to barrenness and weeds.

6

SEPARATED FROM LOT

Is not the whole land before thee?
separate thyself, I pray thee, from me:
if thou wilt take the left hand,
then I will go to the right;
or if thou depart to the right hand,
then I will go to the left.

Genesis 13:9

*I*n our last chapter, we saw something of the original stuff of which God makes His saints. Abraham was not superior by nature to the general run of mankind, who do not hesitate to lie to gain a point or to avert a disaster. The faith that one day was to plow the ocean waves could not swim across a tiny creek. It is hard to imagine that such a man would ever arrive at a stature of moral greatness so commanding as to overshadow his contemporaries and to look across the ages to see the day of Christ. Yet so it was. And from that thought we may take courage.

Our God does not need noble characters as the groundwork of His masterpieces. He who can raise up stones as children can turn thorns into fir trees, briars into myrtle trees. He can take fishermen from their nets and publicans from their tax booths, making them into evangelists, apostles, and martyrs. We are not much by nature—wild, bad blood may be flowing in our veins, but God will be the more magnified if from such stones He can raise up children unto Abraham. The miracle of His grace and power will bring more conspicuous glory to His holy Name, in proportion to the unpromising character of the materials on which He works.

"Abram went up out of Egypt, he, and his wife, and all that he had, and Lot with him, into the south" (Gen. 13:1).

This is very marvelous! Judging by other men, we might have thought that Abraham would never recover from that sad mistake, that disastrous failure and sin. Surely he will reap as he has sown! He will never see his faithful wife again but must bear forever on his conscience the brand of coward treachery! Or if, indeed, she is returned to him, he will never extricate himself from the meshes into which he has thrown himself! Irritated and deceived, Pharaoh will surely find some method of avenging the wrong with which the foreigner has repaid his generous hospitality!

But no. Contrary to all human anticipation, Jehovah appears on the behalf of His most unworthy servant. In later years, the psalmist gives us the very words that God uttered in the heart of the king: "Touch not mine anointed, and do my prophets no harm" (Ps. 105:15). What a marvel of tenderness! God does not cast us away for one sin. "He hath not dealt with us after our sins; nor rewarded us according to our iniquities. For as the heaven is high above the earth, so great is his mercy toward them that fear him" (Ps. 103:10–11). And thus, notwithstanding repeated falls and shortcomings, Jehovah lovingly pursues His divine purpose with the soul in which the "root of the matter" (Job 19:28) is found, until He sets it free from its clinging evils and lifts it into the life of faith and power and familiar friendship with Himself. "Rejoice not against me, O mine enemy: when I fall, I shall arise; when I sit in darkness, the LORD shall be a light unto me" (Micah 7:8).

Warned by this divine voice and restrained by a power that would not allow him to do God's servant harm, Pharaoh "commanded his men concerning him: and they sent him away, and his wife, and all that he had" (Gen. 12:20). This is how it comes to pass that we find them again traversing the uplands of southern Palestine on their way back to Bethel to the place where they had halted on their first entrance into Palestine. So complete was the delivering power of God that the Egyptian monarch did not even take back the gifts that he had bestowed as a dowry for Sarah. The "sheep, and oxen, and he asses, and menservants, and maidservants, and she asses, and camels" (Gen. 12:16) still remained in Abraham's possession. And we are therefore prepared to learn that "Abram was very rich in cattle, in silver, and in gold" (Gen. 13:2). That visit to Egypt beyond a doubt laid the foundation of the immense wealth of the family in later time, and it was out of this that the next trouble sprang. A trouble it seemed at first, but God marvelously overruled it for drawing His child yet closer to Himself, severing the metal to a further extent from the alloy that had clung to it too long. Hitherto, we have been told repeatedly, "and Lot went with him." This record will not be made again.

WHO WAS LOT?

Lot was the son of Abraham's dead brother, Haran. He had probably succeeded to his father's inheritance. While he may have come with his uncle across the desert in the secret hope of bettering his condition, we will hope that he was prompted by worthier motives. He seems to have been one of those men who take right steps, not because they are prompted by obedience to God but because their friends are taking them. Around him was the inspiration of a heroic faith, the fascination of the untried and unknown, and the stir of a great religious movement. Lot was swept into this current and resolved to go, too. He was the Pliable of the earliest Pilgrim's Progress. He may have thought that he was as sincere as Abraham, but it was a great mistake. He was simply an echo, a dim afterglow, a small leaf on the surface of a mighty current.

In every great religious movement there always have been, and always will be, a number of individuals who join up with it, not knowing the power that inspires it. Beware of them! They cannot stand the stress of the life of separation to God. The mere excitement will soon fade away from them, and having no principle to take its place, they will become hindrances and disruptive of the peace. As certainly as they are harbored in the camp or their principles are allowed within the heart, they will lower the spiritual tone, appeal to worldly policy, and suggest methods that would not otherwise occur to us. Thus they draw us toward the Egypt-world.

Nothing but supreme principle can carry anyone through the

real, separated, and surrendered life of the child of God. If you are prompted by anything less, such as excitement, enthusiasm, conformity, or contagious example, you will first be a hindrance, and end by being a failure. Examine yourself, whether you are in the faith. Prove your own self. And if you are consciously acting from a selfish motive, ask God to breathe into you His own pure love. Better act from a lesser motive, if only it is in the right direction, but covet earnestly the best.

THE NECESSITY OF SEPARATION

Abraham's recent failure in connection with Egypt may have been due, to a larger extent than we know, to the unfavorable influence of Lot. Had Abraham been left to himself, he might never have thought of going down to Egypt. In that case, there would have been another paragraph or passage in the Bible describing the exploits of a faith that dared to stand for God's promise, though he was threatened by disaster and hemmed in by famine. Abraham would have been found to be waiting until God should bid him move or make it possible to stay. There is something about that visit to Egypt that savors of the spirit of Lot's later life. In any case, the time had come, in the providence of God, when this more worldly spirit must go its way, leaving Abraham to stand alone, without prop, or adviser, or ally. He was thrown back on the counsel and help of God alone.

The outward separation of the body from the world of the ungodly is incomplete, unless it is accompanied and supplemented by the inner separation of the spirit. It is not enough to leave Ur, Haran, and Egypt. We must be rid of Lot also. Though we lived in a monastery, shut away from the distractions of men, with no sound to break upon the ear but the summoning bell of worship and the solemn chant, yet so long as there was an alien principle in our breast, a Lot in our heart life, there could not be the separation to God that is the condition of the growth of faith and of all those higher forms of the true spiritual life. Lot must go. "Know that the LORD hath set apart him that is godly for himself" (Ps. 4:3). No other foot dare intrude within the courtyard of the divine master.

O souls that sigh for godliness as hearts pant for waterbrooks, have you counted the cost? Can you bear the fiery ordeal? The making of saints is no child's play. The block has to be entirely separated from the mountain bed before the divine chisel can begin to fashion it. The gold must be plunged into the cleansing fire before it can be molded or hammered into an ornament of beauty for the King.

As Abraham was separated from one after another of nature's resources, so it must be with all aspirants for the inner chambers of the palace of God. We must be prepared to die to the world with its criticism or praise, to the flesh with its ambitions and schemes, to the delights of a friendship that is insidiously lowering the temperature of the spirit, to the self-life in all its myriad of subtle and overt manifestations, and even, if it is God's will, to the joys and consolations of religion.

All this is impossible to us by ourselves. But if we will surrender ourselves to God, willing that He should work in and for us that which we cannot do for ourselves, we shall find that He will gradually and effectually, and as tenderly as possible, begin to disentwine the clinging tendrils of the poisoning weed and bring us into heart union with Himself.

It may be that Abraham had already realized the detrimental effect of association with Lot and may have longed to be free from him, without knowing how the emancipation could be effected. In any case, something like this may be the condition of some who shall read these words. Entangled in an alliance that you seem powerless to break off, your only hope is to bear it quietly until God sets you at liberty. Meanwhile, guard your will by God's grace from swinging round as a boat does with the tide. Declare to God continually your eager desire to be free. By prayer and faith get honey out of the lion's carcass. Wait patiently until God's hour strikes and His hand opens the locked door and bids you be free. That time will come at length, for God has a destiny in store for you so great that neither He nor you can allow it to be forfeited for any light or trivial obstacle.

How the Separation Was Brought About

The valleys around Bethel, which had been quite adequate for the entire group's needs when they first arrived in Canaan, were now altogether insufficient. The herdsmen were always wrangling for the first use of the wells and the first crop of the pastures. The cattle were continually getting mixed up. "The land was not able to bear them, that they might dwell together" (Gen. 13:6).

Quarrels between servants have a habit of traveling upward and involving their masters. And so Abraham and Lot would be told by their headmen of what was happening, and each would be tempted to feel irritated with the other.

Abraham saw at once that such a state of things must not be allowed to go on, especially as "the Canaanite and the Perizzite dwelled then in the land" (Gen. 13:7). If those warlike neighbors heard of the dissension in the camp, they would take an early opportunity of falling upon it. United, Abraham and Lot stood; divided, they must fall. Besides, there was the scandal of the thing that might work prejudicial on the name and worship of that God to whom Abraham was known to bow the knee. Would that the close presence of the world might have the same wholesome effect of checking dissension and dispute among the children of the same Father today!

And so Abraham called Lot to him and said, "Let there be no strife, I pray thee, between me and thee, and between my herdmen and thy herdmen; for we be brethren. Is not the whole land before thee? separate thyself, I pray thee, from me: if thou wilt take the left hand, then I will go to the right; or if thou depart to the right hand, then I will go to the left" (Gen. 13:8–9).

The proposal was very *wise*. Abraham saw that there was a cause for the disturbance that would lead to similar troubles continually. If he spoke harshly to Lot, Lot would answer in the same spirit, and a breach would be made at once. So he went to the root of the matter and proposed their separation.

His line of action was very *magnanimous*. As the elder and the leader of the expedition, he had the undoubted right to the first choice. But he waived his right in the interests of reconciliation. But above all, it was *based on faith*. Abraham's faith was beginning to realize its true position and to spread its wings for further and still further flights. Had not God pledged Himself to take care of him and to give him an inheritance? There was no fear, therefore, that Lot could ever rob him of that which was guaranteed to him by the faithfulness of God. And Abraham preferred a thousand times over that God should choose for him than that he should choose for himself.

The man who is sure of God can afford to hold very lightly the things of this world. God Himself is his inalienable heritage, and in having God, he has all. As we shall see, the man who "hedges" for himself does not do so well in the long run as the man who, having the right of choice, hands it back to God, saying: "Let others choose for themselves, if they please. But as for me, You shall choose my inheritance for me."

> Not mine—not mine the choice
>   In things great or small;
> Be Thou my Guide, my Guard, my Strength,
>   My wisdom and my All.

7

THE TWO PATHS

Is not the whole land before thee?
separate thyself, I pray thee, from me.
Genesis 13:9

Abraham and Lot stood together on the heights of Bethel. The land of promise spread out before them as a map. On three sides, at least, there was not much to attract a shepherd's gaze. The eye wandered over the outlines of the hills that hid from view the fertile valleys nestling within their embrace. There was, however, an exception in this monotony of hill country, toward the southeast, where the waters of the Jordan spread out in a broad valley before they entered the Sea of the Plain.

Even from the distance, the two men could discern the rich luxuriance that may have recalled to them traditions of the garden once planted by the Lord God in Eden, reminding them of scenes that they had recently visited together in the valley of the Nile. This especially struck the eye of Lot, who was eager to do the best for himself and determined to make the fullest use of the opportunity that the unexpected magnanimity of his uncle had thrown in his way. Did he count his relative a fool for surrendering the right of choice? Did Lot vow that he must allow no false feelings of tenderness to interfere with his doing what he could for himself? Did he feel strong in the keenness of his sight and the quickness of his judgment? Perhaps so, for he had little sympathy with the pilgrim spirit.

But the time would come when he would bitterly regret his choice and owe everything to the man of whom he was now prepared to take advantage.

"Lot lifted up his eyes, and beheld all the plain of Jordan, that it was well watered every where...even as the garden of the LORD...Then Lot chose him all the plain of Jordan" (Gen. 13:10–11). He did not ask what God had chosen for him. He did not consider the prejudicial effect that the morals of the place might exert upon his children and himself. His choice was entirely determined by the lust of the flesh, the lust of the eyes, and the pride of life. For the "men of Sodom were wicked and sinners before the LORD exceedingly" (Gen. 13:13).

How many have stood upon those Bethel heights, intent on the same errand as Lot! Age after age has poured forth its crowds of young hearts to stand upon an exceeding high mountain, while before them have been spread all the kingdoms of this world and the glory of them. The tempter whispers in their ear that for one act of reverence to him, all shall be theirs. Assured and self-confident, eager to do the very best for themselves, and prepared to consider the moralities only insofar as they did not interfere with what they hold to be the main chance of life, thus have succeeding generations looked toward the plains of Sodom from afar. And alas, like Lot, they have tried to make stones into bread; they have cast themselves down from the mountainside for angels to catch; they have knelt before the tempter, only to find his promise broken, the vision of power an illusion, and the soul bankrupted forever! Meanwhile, the tempter with his hollow laugh has disappeared, leaving his victim standing alone in the midst of a desolate wilderness.

Let us not condemn Lot too much because he chose without regard to the moral and religious conditions of the case, lest, in judging him, we pronounce sentence on ourselves. Lot did nothing more than is done by scores of professing Christians every day.

A Christian man asks you to go over and see the place that he is about to take in the country. It is certainly a charming place. The house is spacious and well situated, the air balmy, the garden and grounds large, the views enchanting. When you have looked it over, you ask how he will fare on Sunday. You put the question not because of curiosity but because you know that he needs strong spiritual influences to counteract the effect of his absorbing business cares from Monday morning till Saturday night, and because you know that his children are beginning to demonstrate a deepening interest in the things of God. "Well," says he, "I really have never thought of it." Or perhaps he answers, "I believe there is nothing here like we have been accustomed to, but one cannot have everything. They say that the society here is extremely good." Is not this the spirit of Lot, who traded the altar of Abraham's camp for the plains of Sodom because the grass looks green and plentiful?

Have mothers never gone into society where evangelical Christianity is held in contempt, for no other reason than to find a good match for their daughters, so far, at least, as the world is concerned? Ah, the world is full of breaking hearts and wrecked happiness because so many persist in lifting up their eyes to choose for themselves with a sole reference to the most shameful considerations.

If Abraham had disputed with Lot, suggesting the mistake he was making, do you not suppose that Lot would have argued: "Do you not think that we are as eager as you are to serve the Lord? Sodom needs just the witness that we shall be able to give. Is it not appropriate that the light should shine in the darkness and that the salt should be scattered where there is decay?" Abraham might not be able to contest these assertions, and yet he would have an inner conviction that these were not the considerations that were determining his nephew's choice. Of course, if God sends a man to Sodom, He will protect him there as Daniel was protected in Babylon. Nothing shall by any means hurt him. He shall be guarded as the eye is guarded in its bony socket from violence and by its delicate veil of eyelid sheltered from the dust. But if God does not clearly send you to Sodom, it is a blunder, a crime, a peril to go.

Note how Lot was swiftly swept into the whirlpool: first he saw; then he chose; then he separated himself from Abraham; then he journeyed east; then he pitched his tent toward Sodom; then he dwelt there; then he became an alderman of the place and sat in the gate. His daughters married two of the men of Sodom, and they probably ranked among the most genteel and influential families of the neighborhood. But his power of a godly witness was gone. Or if he lifted up his voice in protest against deeds of shameless vice, he was laughed at for his pains or threatened with violence. His righteous soul might vex itself, but it met with no sympathy. He was carried captive by Chedorlaomer, and his property was destroyed in the overthrow of the cities. His wife was turned into a pillar of salt, and the blight of Sodom left but too evident a brand upon his daughters. Wretched, indeed, must have been the last days of that pitiable man, cowering in a cave, stripped of everything, face to face with the results of his own shameful sin.

It is, indeed, a terrible picture, and yet a similar retribution is in store for everyone whose choice of home and friends and surroundings is dictated by the lust of worldly gain or fashion or pleasure rather than by the will of God. If such are saved at all, they will be saved as Lot was—so as by fire (1 Cor. 3:15). Now let us turn to a more inviting theme and further consider the dealings of the Almighty God with Abraham, the one man who was being educated to hold fellowship with Jehovah as a friend.

GOD ALWAYS COMES NEAR TO HIS SEPARATED ONES

"And the LORD said unto Abram, *after that Lot was separated from him*" (Gen. 13:14). Perhaps Abraham was feeling very lonely. Lot and he had been constant and close companions. When the last of the camp followers had moved off and Lot had disappeared into the long distance, a cold chill may have enveloped Abraham as a November fog does the man who has arisen before the dawn to see his friend away by the early train. Then it was that God spoke to him.

We all dread to be separated from companions and friends. It is hard to see them stand aloof and drop away one by one as we are compelled to take a course by ourselves. The young girl finds it hard to refuse the evening at the theater and to stay alone at home when her friends have gone off in high spirits. The young city clerk finds it hard to refuse to join in the sweepstake that is being put up on the occasion of some annual race. The merchant finds it hard to withdraw from the club or society with which he has long been identified, despite the realization that practices are creeping in that his conscience refuses to sanction. The Christian teacher finds it hard to adopt a course that isolates him from those with whom he has had sweet fellowship but against whose views he is obliged to protest.

And yet, if we really wish to be only for God, it is inevitable that there will be many links to snap, many companionships to forsake, many habits and standards to drop. Just as a savage must gradually and necessarily reject most of his past before he can be admitted into the society and friendship of his civilized teacher, so must the Christian reject the world.

But let us not stand looking on this aspect of it—the dark side of the cloud. Let us rather catch a glimpse of the other side, illuminated by the rainbow promise of God. And let this be understood, that when the spirit has dared to take up that life of consecration to the will of God to which we are called, there breaks upon it visions, voices, and comfortable words of which the heart could have formed no previous idea. For brass He brings gold, for iron silver, for wood brass, and for stone iron. Violence is no more heard, nor wasting, nor destruction. The sun is no more needed for the day nor the moon for the night, because the Lord has become the everlasting light of the surrendered and separate heart, and the days of its mourning have passed away forever.

"Wherefore come out from among them, and be ye separate, saith the Lord, and touch not the unclean thing; and I will receive you, and will be a Father unto you, and ye shall be my sons and daughters, saith the Lord Almighty. Having therefore these promises, dearly beloved, let us cleanse ourselves from all filthiness of the flesh and spirit" (2 Cor. 6:17—7:1).

GOD WILL DO BETTER FOR THOSE WHO TRUST HIM THAN THEY COULD DO FOR THEMSELVES

Twice here in the context we meet the phrase "lifting up the eyes." But how great the contrast! Lot lifted up his eyes at the dictate of worldly prudence to spy out his own advantage. Abraham lifted up his eyes, not to discern what would best make for his material interests but to behold what God had prepared for him. How much better it is to keep the eye steadfastly fastened on God until

He says to us, "Lift up now thine eyes, and look from the place where thou art northward, and southward, and eastward, and westward: For all the land which thou seest, to thee will I give it, and to thy seed for ever" (Gen. 13:14–15).

God honors those who honor Him. He withholds "no good thing...from them that walk uprightly" (Ps. 84:11). He "meetest him that rejoiceth and worketh righteousness" (Isa. 64:5). If only we will go on doing what is right, giving up the best to our neighbor to avoid dispute, considering God's interests first and our own last, expending ourselves for the coming and glory of the kingdom of heaven, we shall find that God will charge Himself with our interests. And He will do infinitely better for us than we could. Lot had to ask the men of Sodom whether he might sojourn among them, and he had no hold on the land. But it was all given unasked to Abraham, including that verdant circle on which Lot had set his heart. "Blessed are the meek: for they shall inherit the earth" (Matt. 5:5).

It is difficult to read these glowing words, *northward, and southward, and eastward, and westward*, without being reminded of "the breadth, and length, and depth, and height; and to know the love of Christ, which passeth knowledge" (Eph. 3:18–19). Much of the land of Canaan was hidden behind the ramparts of the hills, but enough was seen to ravish that faithful spirit. Similarly, we may not be able to comprehend the love of God in Christ, but the higher we climb, the more we behold. The upper elevations of the separated life command the fullest view of that measureless expanse.

In some parts of the western Highlands of Scotland, the traveler's eye is delighted by the clear and sunlit waters of a loch—an arm of the sea running far up into the hills. But as he climbs over the heathery slopes and catches sight of the waters of the Atlantic, bathed in the light of the setting sun, he almost forgets the fair vision that had just arrested him. Thus do growing elevation and separation of character unfold ever richer conceptions of Christ's infinite love and character.

God's promises are ever on the ascending scale. One leads up to another, fuller and more blessed than itself. In Mesopotamia, God said, "I will show thee the land." At Bethel, "This is the land." Here, "I will give thee all the land, and children innumerable as the grains of sand." And we shall find even these eclipsed. It *is* thus that God charms us to saintliness. Not giving anything until we have dared to act—that He may test us. Not giving everything at first—that He may not overwhelm us. And always keeping in hand an infinite reserve of blessing. Oh, the unexplored remainders of God! Who ever saw His last star?

GOD BIDS US APPROPRIATE HIS GIFTS

"Arise, walk through the land in the length of it and in the breadth of it" (Gen. 13:17). This surely means that God wished Abraham to feel as free in the land as if the title deeds were actually in his hands. Abraham was to enjoy the land, to travel through it, and to look upon it as his own. By faith, Abraham was to act toward it as if he were already in absolute possession.

There is a deep lesson here as to the appropriation of faith. "Be strong and very courageous" was addressed six times to Joshua. "Be strong" refers to the strength of the wrists to grasp. "Be very courageous" refers to the tenacity of the ankle joints to hold their ground. May our faith be strong in each of these particulars. Strong to lay hold, and strong to keep.

The difference between Christians consists in this. For us all there are equal reserves of spiritual blessing laid up in our Lord, but some of us have learned more constantly and fully to appropriate them. We walk through the land in its lengths and breadths. We avail ourselves of the fullness of Jesus. Not content with what He is for us in the counsel of God, our constant appeal is to Him in every moment of need.

We need not be surprised to learn that Abraham moved to Hebron (which signifies *fellowship*) and built there an altar to the Lord. New mercies call us to deeper fellowship with our Almighty Friend, who never leaves or forsakes His own. And as the result of His dealings with us, let us build fresh altars and make a new dedication of ourselves and all we have to His blessed service.

8

REFRESHMENT BETWEEN THE BATTLES

Four kings with five.
Genesis 14:9

*T*he strife recorded in Genesis 14 was no mere border foray. It was an expedition for punishment and conquest. Chedorlaomer was the Attila, the Napoleon of his age. His capital city, Susa, lay across the desert, beyond the Tigris in Elam. Years before Abraham had entered Canaan as a peaceful emigrant, this dreaded conqueror had swept southward, subduing the towns that lay in the Jordan Valley, and thus he held the master key to the road between Damascus and Memphis. When Lot took up his residence toward Sodom, the cities of the plain were paying tribute to this mighty monarch.

At last the men of Sodom and Gomorrah, of Admah and Zeboiim, became weary of the Elamite yoke and rebelled, and Chedorlaomer was compelled to undertake a second expedition to chastise their revolt and regain his power. Combining his own forces with those of three vassal and friendly rulers in the Euphrates Valley, which lay in his way, he swept across the desert and fell upon the wild tribes that harbored in the mountains of Bashan and Moab. His plan was evidently to ravage the whole country contiguous to those Jordan towns before actually investing them.

At last the allied forces concentrated in the neighborhood of Sodom, where they encountered fierce resistance. Encouraged by the pitchy nature of the soil, in which horsemen and chariots would move with difficulty, the townsfolk risked an engagement in the open. In spite, however, of the bitumen pits, the day went against the depraved men of the plain, in whose case, as in many others, social corruption proved itself the forerunner of political overthrow. The defeat of the troops was followed by the capture and plunder of those wealthy towns; and all who could not escape were manacled as slaves and carried off by the victorious army.

Satisfied at length with their success, their attention engrossed by their rich booty and their vast host of captives, the foreign host began slowly to return along the Jordan Valley on its homeward march. "And they took Lot, Abram's brother's son, who dwelt in Sodom, and his goods, and departed" (Gen. 14:12). Then one of the survivors of that fatal day climbed the hills and made for Abraham's encampment, which he may have known in earlier days when, as one of Lot's many servants, he lived there. "And when Abram heard that his brother was taken captive, he armed his trained servants...and he divided himself against them" (Gen. 14:14–15).

ABRAHAM'S INTERVENTION ON THE BEHALF OF OTHERS

Hidden in the configuration of the country and allied with his friends, Abraham had watched the movements of the devastators from afar. "But it shall not come nigh thee. Only with thine eyes shalt thou behold and see the reward of the wicked" (Ps. 91:7–8). Common prudence would have urged him to not involve himself. No doubt someone said to Abraham, "Be thankful that you have escaped. Do not meddle further in the business, lest you make these mighty kings your foes."

But true separation to God never argues thus. Granted that the separated one is set apart for God, yet he is set apart that he may react more efficiently on the great world over which God yearns and toward which He has entertained great purposes of mercy in the election of the few. Genuine separation—a detachment from the things of time and reason because of an ardent devotion to the unseen and eternal—is the result of faith that always works by love, and this love tenderly yearns for those who are entangled in the meshes of worldliness and sin. Faith makes us independent but not indifferent. It is enough for it to hear that its brother is taken captive, and it will arm instantly to go in pursuit.

Ah, brothers and sisters, have there never come to you the tidings that your brothers are taken captive? How, then, is it that you have not started off long ago for their deliverance? Is a separation to God genuine that can stand by unconcerned while there is such need for immediate and unselfish action?

But Abraham's intervention was as *successful* as it was unselfish and prompt. The force with which he set out was a very small one, but his raw recruits moved quickly. Thus in four or five days they overtook the self-reliant and encumbered host amid the hills where the Jordan takes its rise. Adopting the tactics of a night attack, he suddenly came against the unsuspecting host and chased them in headlong panic as far as the ancient city of Damascus. "And he brought back all the goods, and also brought again his brother Lot, and his goods, and the women also, and the people" (Gen. 14:16).

Is this not always so? The men who live the life of separation and devotion toward God are the ones who act with the most promptness and success when the time for action comes. Lot, being in Sodom, could neither elevate its morals nor save it from attack. Abraham, living among the hills, is alone able to cope successfully with the might of the tyrant king. Oh, do not listen to those who say you must live at the same level and in the midst of worldly men in order to elevate and save them, advising you to participate in worldly affairs in order to give them a higher tone. Did Lot save Sodom? Nor will a better fate than his befall any man who, unbidden by God, settles down in the world for his own whim and pleasure. If you would lift me, you must stand above me. If Archimedes is to move the world, he must rest his lever on a point far enough outside the earth itself.

GREAT SUCCESS OFTEN
WARNS OF GREAT TEMPTATION

The King of Sodom had not been among the prisoners. He had probably saved himself by a timely flight to the hills from the field of battle. When therefore he received the news of the patriarch's gallant and successful expedition, the king set out to meet and welcome him. He would ascend from the Jordan plain by one of the gorges into the hills and come out on the great central road by which Abraham and his allies were marching back to Hebron.

The two met at the king's dale, a place to become memorable as the years went on (2 Sam. 18:18) and situated near the city of Salem, a title that was destined to develop into the word Jerusalem. It was a memorable meeting between the representatives of two races—the one destined to grow weaker and weaker until it was dispossessed by the children of that very man whose sword now saved it from utter extinction.

More memorable than the place is the record of the spiritual encounter that took place there. Grateful for Abraham's help and deliverance, the King of Sodom proposed that Abraham surrender only the persons of the captives while he kept all the spoils to himself and his allies. It must have been a very tempting offer. It was no slight matter for a shepherd to have the chance of appropriating all the spoils of settled townships, so large and prosperous, especially when he seemed to have some claim on them. But Abraham would not hear of it for a moment. Indeed, he seems to have already undergone some exercise of soul on the matter, for speaking as of a past transaction, he said, "I have lift up mine hand unto the LORD, the most high God, the possessor of heaven and earth, that I will not take from a thread even to a shoelatchet, and that I will not take any thing that is thine, lest thou shouldst say, I have made Abram rich" (Gen. 14:22–23). What a magnificent contempt of the special offer! What a glorious outburst of the independence of a living faith!

A close parallel exists between this suggestion of the King of Sodom and the temptation of our Lord in the wilderness when Satan offered Him all the kingdoms of the world for one act of obeisance (Matt. 4). And does not this temptation assail us all? Are we not all tempted to take the gilded wage of the world that is so eager to put us under obligation to itself and to feel that we are in its pay and power? The world is aware that if we will only accept its subsidies, we shall have surrendered our position of independence and stepped down to its level, no longer able to witness against it, shorn of the locks of our strength and become weak as other men.

In theory it may be argued that we can turn to good account the wealth that has been gotten from the world. But practically, we shall not find it so. The wealth of Sodom will scorch the hand that handles it, blighting every godly enterprise to which it may be put. Besides, what right have we to depend on the revenues of the world? We are heirs to the Possessor of heaven and earth, the children of the Great King. In giving us His Son, He has also pledged to give us all things. Better a thousand times to be poor until He make us rich with the gold that has passed through His cleansing furnace. Happy are they who prefer to live on the daily providence of God to being dependent on the gold of Sodom—the wages of iniquity.

THE PREVENIENT GRACE OF GOD

It may be that Abraham would not have come off so grandly in the second conflict if he had not been prepared for it by the wondrous encounter with a greater king than either we have named. After his defeat of Chedorlaomer and before the advent of the king of Sodom, the Hebrew had met Melchizedek, the priest-king of Salem.

We may not stay to speak now of all the interest that gathers around this sacred figure, sacred as the type of our blessed Lord. We shall be satisfied to notice now that he brought bread and wine and blessed the weary conqueror and coined in his hearing a new name for God. For the first time God received the title, "Possessor of heaven and earth" (Gen. 14:19)—one that seems to have made a deep impression upon Abraham, for we find him using it in his encounter with the King of Sodom. It was the icon of victory. Why should Abraham need to take possessions from man when this new revelation of God had just fallen upon his ear and enriched his heart forever?

Is not this the work of the Lord Jesus still? He comes to us when we are wearily returning from the fight. He comes to us when He knows we are on the eve of a great temptation. He not only prays for us, as for Peter, but also prepares us for the conflict. Some new revelation, some fresh glimpse into His character, some holy thought—these are given to fill the memory and heart against the advent of the foe. Oh, matchless mercy! He forewarns and forearms us. He prepares us with the blessings of His goodness.

When next we are tempted with the bribes of an ungodly world, let us recall that name for God, which, in Abraham's case, was the icon of victory. Let us think of God as the possessor of heaven and earth. Why should we soil our fingers with ill-gotten gains, even though they seem needful for our existence, when our Father is the Owner of all that flies in the air, treads on the land, swims in the water, or lies embedded in the rocks.

We have often been made sweet and strong or have passed through some marked spiritual experience for no other reason than to equip us for coming peril. Let us avail ourselves of such occasions whenever they occur, and let us ever be grateful to our Lord for provisioning His castles before they are attacked and for giving us His own new name by which we may overcome all the wiles of men and devils.

O King of loyal hearts, may we meet You more often on life's highway, especially when some tempter is preparing to weave around us the meshes of evil. And bending beneath Your blessing, may we be prepared by the communications of Your grace for all that may await us in the unknown future!

9

MELCHIZEDEK

For this Melchizedek, King of Salem,
priest of the most high God.
Hebrews 7:1

*C*hrist is here! The passage is fragrant with the ointment of His name. Our hands drip with myrrh and our fingers with sweet-smelling myrrh as we lay them upon the handles of this lock (Song of Sol. 5:5). Let us get aside from the busy rush of life and think long, deep thoughts of Him who is the Alpha and the Omega of Scripture and of saintly hearts. And let us draw from the unsearchable depths of His nature, by the bucket of this mysterious record touching Melchizedek, the king of Salem.

There is a sense in which Christ was made *after the order of Melchizedek*, but there is a deeper sense in which Melchizedek was made *after the order of the Son of God*. The writer to the Hebrews tells us that Melchizedek was "made like unto the Son of God" (Heb. 7:3). Christ is the Archetype of all and from all eternity has had those qualities that have made Him so much to us. It would seem as if they could not wait to be manifested in the fullness of the ages; they chafed for expression. From of old, His delights were with the sons of men. And so this mysterious royal priest was constituted—reigning in his peaceful city amid the storm and wreckage of his times—that there might be given among men some clue and anticipation of that glorious life that was already being lived in heaven on man's behalf and which, in due course, would be manifested on our world and at that very spot where Melchizedek lived his Christlike life. Oh, that we, too, might be priests after the order of Melchizedek in this respect, if in no other, that we are made as much as possible to the Son of God!

MELCHIZEDEK WAS A PRIEST

The spiral column of smoke climbing up into the clear air—in the fragrant morn and again at the dewy eve—told that there was one heart at least that was true in its allegiance to the Most High God. Here was one who bore up before Him the sins and sorrows of the clans that clustered near. He seems to have had that quick sympathy with the needs of his times that is the true mark of the priestly heart (Heb. 4:15). And he had acquired thereby so great an influence over his neighbors that they spontaneously acknowledged the claims of his special and unique position. Man must have a priest. His nature shrinks from contact with the All Holy. What is there in common between vileness and purity, darkness and light, ignorance and the knowledge that needs no telling? And in all ages, men have selected from among their fellows one who should represent them to God, and God to them. It is a natural instinct. And it has been met in our glorious Lord, who, while He stands for us in the presence of God, face to face with uncreated Light, ever making intercessions, at the same time is touched with the feeling of our infirmities, helps us in our temptations, and has compassion on our ignorance. Why need we travel farther afield? Why imitate Micah in setting up for ourselves a priest whom human hands have made (Judges 17:10–12)? Why permit any other to bear this sacred name or to intrude on this holy office? None but Christ will satisfy or meet the requirements of God or "become us" with unutterable needs (Heb. 7:26).

A Priesthood from God and Ratified by an Oath

The priests of the house of Levi exercised their office after "the law of a carnal commandment" (Heb. 7:16). They assumed the priesthood, not because of any inherent ability or because they were specially summoned to the work by the voice of heaven but because they had sprung from the special priestly tribe. The Priesthood of Christ, on the other hand, is God's best gift to men—to you, my reader, and to me. It is more necessary than spring flowers or light or air. Without it our souls would wander ever in a Sahara desert. "Christ glorified not himself to be made an high priest" (Heb. 5:5), but He was called of God to be a High Priest after the order of Melchizedek (Heb. 5:10). And such was the solemnity of His appointment, that it was ratified by "the word of the oath" (Heb. 7:28). "The Lord sware and will not repent, Thou art a priest for ever, after the order of Melchizedek" (Heb. 7:21). Here is "strong consolation" indeed. No unfaithfulness or ingratitude can change this priesthood. The eternal God will never run back from that word and oath. "Eternity" is written upon the High Priest's brow: "forevermore" rings out from the chime of His golden bells as He moves. "An unchangeable priesthood" (Heb. 7:24) is the law of His glorious being. Hallelujah! The heart may well sing, when, amid the fluctuation of earth's change, it touches at length the primeval rock of God's eternal purpose. He is "consecrated" Priest "for evermore" (Heb. 7:28).

A Universal Priesthood

Abraham was not yet circumcised. He was not a Jew, but a Gentile still. It was as the father of many nations that he stood and worshiped and received the benediction from Melchizedek's saintly hands. Not thus was it with the priesthood of Aaron's line. To share its benefit a man must become a Jew, submitting to the initial rite of Judaism. None but Jewish names shone in that breastplate. Only Jewish needs or sins were borne upon those consecrated lips. But Christ is the Priest of man. He draws *all men* to Himself. The one sufficient claim upon Jesus Christ is that you bear the nature that He has taken into irreversible union with His own—that you are a penitent sinner pressed by conscious need. Then you have a right to Him that cannot be disallowed. He is your Priest—your own, as if none other had claim on Him than you. Tell Him all your story, hiding nothing, excusing nothing. All kindreds and peoples and nations and tongues converge and are welcome in Jesus Christ, and all their myriad needs are satisfactorily met.

A SUPERIOR PRIESTHOOD

If ever there was a priesthood that held undisputed supremacy among the priesthoods of the world, it was that of Aaron's line. It might not be as ancient as that which ministered at the shrines of Nineveh or so learned as that which was exercised in the silent Egyptian cloisters of Memphis and Thebes, but it had about it this unapproachable dignity—that it emanated, as a whole, from the Word of God. Yet even the Aaronic priesthood must yield obeisance to the Melchizedek priesthood. And it did. For Levi was yet in the loins of Abraham when Melchizedek met him, and Levi paid tithes in Abraham and knelt in token of submission in the person of the patriarch, beneath the blessing of this greater than himself (Heb. 7:4–10). Why, then, should we concern ourselves with the stars when the sun has arisen upon us? What have we to do with any other than with this mighty Mediator, this Daysman, who towers far above all rivals. Jesus is Himself sacrifice and Priest, who has offered a solitary sacrifice and fulfills a unique ministry!

THIS PRIESTHOOD PARTOOK
OF THE MYSTERY OF ETERNITY

We need not suppose that this mystic being had literally no father or mother, beginning of days or end of life. The fact on which the inspired writer fixes is that no information is given regarding any of these points. There is an intention in the golden silence as well as in the golden speech of Scripture. And these details were doubtless shrouded in obscurity that there might be a still clearer analogy to the glory of the Antitype, who abides continually. He is the Ancient of Days, the King of the Ages, the great I AM. The Sun of His Being, like His Priesthood, knows nothing of dawn, or decline from meridian ascendancy, or descent in the western sky. "[He] is made...after the power of an endless life" (Heb. 7:16). ."He ever liveth to make intercession for them" (Heb. 7:25). If, in John's vision of Patmos, the hair of His head was white as snow, it was not the white of decay but of incandescent fire. "He continueth ever, hath an unchangeable priesthood" (Heb. 7:24). "Jesus Christ the same yesterday, and to day, and for ever" (Heb. 13:8). He does for us now what He did for the world's gray fathers, and what He will do for the last sinner who shall claim His aid.

THIS PRIESTHOOD WAS ROYAL

"Melchizedek, king of Salem, priest" (Heb. 7:1). Here again there is no analogy in the Levitical priesthood.

The royal and priestly offices were carefully kept apart. Uzziah was struck with the white brand of leprosy when he tried to unite them (2 Chron. 26:16–21). But how marvelously they blended in the earthly life of Jesus! As Priest, He pitied and helped and fed men. As King, He ruled the waves. As Priest, He uttered His sublime intercessory prayer. As King, He spoke the "I will" of royal prerogative. As Priest, He touched the ear of Malchus. As the disowned King, to whom even Caesar was preferred, He was hounded to the death. As Priest, He pleaded for His murderers and spoke of paradise to the dying thief, while His Kingship was attested by the proclamation affixed to His cross. As Priest, He breathed peace on His disciples. As King, He ascended to sit down upon His throne.

He was *first* "King of righteousness," and after that also King of Salem, which, is King of Peace" (Heb. 7:2). Mark the order. Not first peace at any price or at the cost of righteousness, but righteousness first—both the righteousness of His personal character and the righteous meeting, on our behalf, of the just demands of a divine and holy law. And then founded on and arising from this solid and indestructible basis, there sprang the Temple of Peace, in which the souls of men may shelter from the shocks of time. "The work of righteousness shall be peace; and the effect of righteousness quietness and assurance for ever. And my people shall dwell in a peaceable habitation, and in sure dwellings, and in quiet resting places" (Isa. 32:17–18).

Ah, dear soul, what is your attitude toward Him? There are many people who are willing enough to have Him as Priest but who refuse to accept Him as King. But it will not do. He must be King or He will not be Priest. And He must be King in this order, first making you right with God, then giving you His peace that passes all understanding. Waste not precious time in arguing with Him; accept the situation as it is, and let your heart be the Salem, the city of Peace, where He, the Priest-King, shall reign forever. And none is so worthy to rule as He who stooped to die. "In the midst of the throne...stood a Lamb as it had been slain" (Rev. 5:6). Exactly! The throne is the befitting place for the Man who loved us to the death.

THIS PRIESTHOOD RECEIVES TITHES OF ALL

"The patriarch Abraham gave the tenth of the spoils" (Heb. 7:4). This ancient custom shames us Christians. The patriarch gave more to the representative of Christ than many of us give to Christ Himself. Come, if you have never done so before, resolve to give your Lord a tithe of your time, your income, your all. "Bring ye all the tithes into the storehouse" (Mal. 3:10). No, You glorious One, we will not rest content with this; take all, for all is Yours. "Thine, O LORD, is the greatness, and the power, and the glory, and the victory, and the majesty: for all that is in the heaven and in the earth is thine; thine is the kingdom, O LORD, and thou art exalted as head above all.... Now therefore, our God, we thank thee, and praise thy glorious name" (1 Chron. 29:11, 13).

10

THE FIRMNESS OF ABRAHAM'S FAITH

He staggered not at the promise of God through unbelief;
but was strong in faith, giving glory to God.
Romans 4:20

*I*n Genesis 15, for the first time in Scripture, four striking phrases occur, but each of them is destined to be frequently repeated with many charming variations. We may speak, then, of its precious paragraphs as of some upland valley where streams take their rise that are to flow seaward, making glad the lowland pasturelands on their way. Now, first, we meet the phrase, "the word of the LORD came" (vs. 1). Here, first, we are told that the Lord God is a shield (vs. 1). For the first time rings out the silver chime of that divine assurance, "Fear not!" (vs. 1). And now we first meet in human history that great, that mighty word, *believed* (vs. 6). What higher glory is there for man than that he should believe in the faithfulness of God? For this is the meaning of all true belief.

The word of the Lord came to Abraham about two distinct matters.

GOD SPOKE TO ABRAHAM ABOUT HIS FEAR

Abraham had just returned from the rout of Chedorlaomer and the confederate kings in the far north of Canaan. He was about to face a natural reaction to the long and unusual strain as he settled down again into the placid and uneventful course of a shepherd's life. In this state of mind he was most susceptible to fear, much like how a weakened body is most susceptible to disease.

There was good reason for fear. Abraham had defeated Chedorlaomer, it is true, but in doing so, he had made him his bitter foe. The arm of the warrior king had been long enough to reach to Sodom. Why should it not be long enough and strong enough to avenge his defeat upon that one lonely man? It could not be believed that the mighty monarch would be content until the memory of his disastrous defeat was wiped out with blood. There was every reason, therefore, to expect Chedorlaomer back again to inflict a revengeful punishment. And besides all this, as a night wind in a desert land, there swept now and again over the heart of Abraham a feeling of lonely desolation, of disappointment, of hope deferred. More than ten years had passed since Abraham had entered Canaan. Three successive promises had kindled his hopes, but they seemed as far from realization as ever. Not one inch of territory! Not a sign of a child! Nothing of all that God had foretold!

It was under such circumstances that the word of the Lord came to him, saying, "Fear not, Abram: I am thy shield, and thy exceeding great reward." Ah, our God does not always wait for us to come to Him. He often comes to us. He draws near to us in the low dungeon. He sends His angel to prepare for us the cruse of water and the baken cakes, and over our souls break His tender assurances of comfort, more penetrating than the roar of the surge, "Be of good cheer; it is I; be not afraid" (Matt. 14:27; Mark 6:50).

But God does not content Himself with vague assurances. He gives us solid ground for comfort in some fresh revelation of Himself. And often the very circumstances of our need are chosen as a contrast to set forth some special side of the divine character that is peculiarly appropriate. What could have been more reassuring at this moment to the defenseless pilgrim, who had no stockade or walled city in which to shelter and whose flocks were scattered far and wide, than to hear that God Himself was around him as a vast, impenetrable though invisible shield. "I am thy shield."

Mankind, when once that promise was given, eagerly took hold of it, and it has never been allowed to die. Again and again it rings out in prophecy and psalms, in temple anthem and from retired musings. "For the Lord God is a sun and shield" (Ps. 84:11). "Thou art my hiding place and my shield" (Ps. 119:114). "Behold, O God our shield, and look upon the face of thine anointed" (Ps. 84:9). "His truth shall be thy shield and buckler" (Ps. 91:4). It is a very helpful thought for some of us! We go every day into the midst of danger where men and devils strike at us—now it is the overt attack, then the stab of the assassin; unkind insinuations, evil suggestions, taunts, gibes, threats. All these things are against us. But if we are doing God's will and trusting in God's care, ours is a charmed life, like that of the man who wears chain armor beneath his clothes. The divine presence surrounds us, rendering us impenetrable to attack. "No weapon that is formed against thee shall prosper" (Isa. 54:17). "Thou shalt not be afraid for the terror by night; nor for the arrow that flieth by day; nor for the pestilence that walketh in darkness; nor for the destruction that wasteth at noonday. A thousand shall fall at thy side, and ten thousand at thy right hand; but it shall not come nigh thee" (Ps. 91:5–7). Happy are they who have learned the art of abiding within the hallowed protection of the eternal God, on which all arrows are blunted, all swords turned aside, all fires of malice extinguished with the hissing sound of a torch in the briny waters of the sea.

Nor does God only defend us from without, for He is the *reward* and satisfaction of the lonely heart. It was as if He asked Abraham to consider how much he had in having Himself. "Come now, my child, and consider. Even if you were never to have one foot of soil and your tent were to stand silent amid the merry laughter of childish voices all around, yet you would not have left your land in vain, for you have Me. Am I not enough? I fill heaven and earth; cannot I fill one lonely soul? Am I not your exceeding great reward, able to compensate you with My friendship for any sacrifice that you may have made?"

Our God, who is love, and love in its purest, divinest essence, has given us much, and promised us more. But still His best and greatest gift is His own dear self—our reward, our great reward, our exceeding great reward. Have you not received Him? Is your life barren? Have lover and friend forsaken you? Are you lonely and forsaken of all the companions of younger days? Well, answer this one question: Is God yours? For if you have Him, you have all love and life, all sweetness and tenderness, all that can satisfy the heart and delight the mind. All lovely things sleep in Him, as all colors hide in the sunbeam's ray, waiting to be unraveled. To have God is to have all, though bereft of everything. To be destitute of God is to be bereft of everything, though having all.

GOD SPOKE TO ABRAHAM ABOUT HIS CHILDLESSNESS

It was night, or perhaps the night was turning toward the morning, but as yet myriads of stars—the watchfires of the angels, the choristers of the spheres, the flocks on the wide pasturelands of space—were sparkling in the heavens. The patriarch was sleeping in his tent when God came near him in a vision, and it was under the shadow of that vision that Abraham was able to tell God all that was in his heart. We can often say things in the dark that we dare not utter beneath the eye of day. And in that quiet watch of the night, Abraham poured out into the ear of God the bitter, bitter agony of his heart's life. He had probably long wanted to say something like this, but the opportunity had not come. But now there was no longer need for restraint, and so it all came right out into the ear of his Almighty Friend. "Behold, to me thou hast given no seed: and, lo, one born in my house is mine heir" (Gen. 15:3). It was as if he said, "I promised for myself something more than this. I have considered Your promises and felt that they surely spoke of a child of my own flesh and blood. But the slow-moving years have brought me no fulfillment of my hopes, and I suppose that I mistook You. You never intended more than that my steward should inherit my name and possessions. Ah, me! It is a bitter disappointment, but You have done it, and it is good."

So we often mistake God and interpret His delays as denials. What a chapter might be written of God's delays! Was not the life of Jesus full of them, from the moment when He stayed behind in the Temple to the moment when He abode two days still in the same place where He was, instead of hurrying across the Jordan in response to the sad and agonized request of the sisters whom He loved. So He delays still. It is the mystery of the art of educating human spirits to the finest quality of which they are capable. What searchings of heart, what analyzing of motives, what testings of the word of God; what upliftings of soul—searching what, or what manner of time, the Spirit of God signifies! All these are associated with those weary days of waiting that are nevertheless laden with spiritual destiny. But such delays are not God's final answer to the soul that trusts Him. They are but the winter before the burst of spring. "And, behold, the word of the LORD came unto him, saying, This shall not be thine heir; but he that shall come forth out of thine own bowels shall be thine heir.... Look now toward heaven, and tell the stars, if thou be able to number them: and he said unto him, So shall thy seed be" (Gen. 15:4–5). And from that moment, the stars shone with new meaning for him as the sacraments of divine promise.

"AND HE BELIEVED IN THE LORD"

Little wonder that those words are so often quoted by inspired men in later ages. They lie as the foundation stone of some of the greatest arguments that have ever engaged the mind of man! (See Rom. 4:3; Gal. 3:6; James 2:23.)

HE BELIEVED BEFORE HE UNDERWENT CIRCUMCISION

The apostle Paul lays special emphasis on this, as showing that they who were not Jews might equally have faith and be numbered among the spiritual children of the great father of the faithful (Rom. 4:9–21; Gal. 3:7–29). The promise that Abraham should be the heir of the world was made to him when he was still only the far-traveled pilgrim. And so it is sure to all the seed, not to that only which is of the law but to that also which is of the faith of Abraham, who is the father of us all.

HE BELIEVED IN FACE OF STRONG IMPROBABILITIES

Appearances were dead against such a thing as the birth of a child to that aged pair. The experience of many years said, "It cannot be." The nature and reason of the case said, "It cannot be." Any council of human friends and advisers would have instantly said, "It cannot be!" And Abraham quietly considered and weighed them all "being not weak in faith" (Rom. 4:19). Then he as carefully looked to the promise of God. And rising from his consideration of the comparative weight of the one and the other, he elected to venture everything on the word of the Eternal. No, that was not all. As shock followed shock and wave succeeded wave, booming with the crash of thunder on his soul, he staggered not; he did not budge an inch; he did not even tremble, as sometimes the wave-beat rock shivers to its base. He counted on the faithfulness of God. He gave glory to God. He relied implicitly on the utter trustworthiness of the divine veracity. He was "fully persuaded that, what he had promised, he was able also to perform" (Rom. 4:21). Ah, child of God, for every look at the unlikelihood of the promise, take ten looks at the promise: this is the way in which faith grows strong. "He staggered not at the promise of God through unbelief; but was strong in faith, giving glory to God" (Rom. 4:20).

HIS FAITH WAS DESTINED TO BE SEVERELY TRIED

If you take to the lapidary the stones that you have collected in your summer wanderings, he will probably send the bulk of them home to you in a few days with scanty marks of having passed through his hands. But one or two of the number may be kept back, and when you inquire for them, he will reply: "The stones that I returned are not worth much. There was nothing in them to warrant the expenditure of my time and skill; but with the others, the case is far otherwise. They are capable of taking a polish and of bearing a discipline that it may take months and even years to give. But their beauty, when the process is complete, will be all the compensation that can be wished."

Some men pass through life without much trial because their natures are light and trivial. They are incapable of bearing much or of profiting by the severe discipline that, in the case of others, is all needed and will yield a rich recompense after it has had its perfect work. God will not let us be tried beyond what we are able to bear. But when He has in hand a nature like Abraham's, which is capable of the loftiest results, we must not be surprised if the trial is long continued, almost to the final limit of endurance. The patriarch had to wait fifteen years more, making twenty-five years in all between the first promise and its fulfillment in the birth of Isaac.

HIS FAITH WAS COUNTED TO HIM FOR RIGHTEOUSNESS

Faith is the seed of righteousness, and when God sees us possessed of the seed, He counts us as also being in possession of the harvest that lies hidden in its heart. Faith is the tiny seed that contains all the rare perfumes and gorgeous hues of the Christian life, awaiting only the nurture and benediction of God. When a man believes, it is only a matter of training and time to develop that which is already in embryo within him; and God, to whom the future is already present, accounts the man of faith as gifted with the fruits of righteousness, which are to the glory and praise of God. But there is a deeper meaning still than this—in the possession through faith of a judicial righteousness in the sight of God.

The righteousness of Abraham resulted not from his works but from his faith. "Abraham believed God, and it was accounted to him for righteousness" (Gal. 3:6). "Now it was not written for his sake alone, that it was imputed to him; but for us also, to whom it shall be imputed, if we believe on him that raised up Jesus our Lord from the dead" (Rom. 4:23–24). Oh, miracle of grace! If we trust ever so simply in Jesus Christ our Lord, we shall be reckoned as righteous in the eye of the eternal God. We cannot realize all that is included in those marvelous words. This much is absolutely evident: faith unites us so absolutely to the Son of God that we are one with Him forevermore; and all the glory of His character—not only what He was when He became obedient unto death but also what He is in the majesty of His risen nature—is reckoned unto us.

Some teach imputed righteousness as if it were something apart from Christ, flung over the rags of the sinner. But it is truer and better to consider it as a matter of blessed identification with Him through faith, so that as He was one with us in being made sin, we are one with Him in being made the righteousness of God. In the counsels of eternity, that which is true of the glorious Lord is accounted also true of us who, by a living faith, have become members of His body, of His flesh, and of His bones. Jesus Christ is made unto us righteousness, and we are accepted in the Beloved. There is nothing in faith, considered in itself, that can account for this marvelous fact of imputation. Faith is only the link of union, but inasmuch as it unites us to the Son of God, it brings us into the enjoyment of all that He is as the Alpha and the Omega, the Beginning and the End, the First and the Last.

11

WATCHING
WITH GOD

*And he said unto him, I am the LORD that brought thee out
of Ur of the Chaldees, to give thee this land to inherit it.*

Genesis 15:7

*For the vision is yet for an appointed time, but at the end it shall speak, and not
lie: though it tarry, wait for it; because it will surely come, it will not tarry.*

Habakkuk 2:3

*It is good that a man should both hope
and quietly wait for the salvation of the LORD.*

Lamentations 3:26

But if we hope for that we see not, then do we with patience wait for it.

Romans 8:25

*I*t is not easy to watch with God or to wait for
Him. The orbit of His providence is so vast. The stages of His
progress are so wide apart. He holds on His way through the ages;
we tire in a few short hours. And when His dealings with us are per-
plexing and mysterious, the heart that had boasted its unwavering
loyalty begins to tire with misgivings and to question. When will we
be able to trust absolutely and not be afraid?

In human relationships, when the heart finds its rest and trust
in another, it can bear the test of distance and delay. Years may pass
without a word or sigh to break the sad monotony. Strange contra-
dictions may baffle the understanding and confuse the mind.
Impertinent friends may delight in putting unkind and false con-
structions on conduct that is confessedly hard to explain. But the

trust never varies or abates. It knows that all is well. It is content to exist without a sign and to be quiet without attempting to explain or defend. Ah, when shall we treat God like this? When shall we thus rest in Him, trusting where we cannot understand? Can any training be too hard that shall secure this as its final and crowning result? Surely that were heaven, when the heart of man could afford to wait for a millennium, unstaggered by delay, untinged by doubt.

At this stage, at least, of his schooling, Abraham had not learned this lesson. But in that gray dawn, as the stars that symbolized his posterity were beginning to fade in the sky, he answered the divine assurance that he should inherit the land of which he as yet did not own a foot, by the sad complaint: "LORD GOD, whereby shall I know that I shall inherit it?" (Gen. 15:8).

How human this is! It was not that he was absolutely incredulous, but he yearned for some tangible sign that it was to be as God had said. He wanted something he could see, something that should be an ever-present sacrament of the coming heritage, as the stars were of the future seed. Do not wonder at him, but rather adore the love that bears with these human frailties and stoops to give them stepping stones by which to cross the sands to the firm rock of an assured faith.

WATCHING BY THE SACRIFICE

In those early days, when a written agreement was very rare, if not quite unknown, men sought to bind one another to their word with the most solemn religious sanctions. The contracting party was required to bring certain animals that were to be slaughtered and divided into pieces. These were laid on the ground in such a manner as to leave a narrow lane between them, up and down which the covenanting party passed to ratify and confirm his solemn pledge.

It was to this ancient and solemn rite that Jehovah referred when He said, "Take me an heifer of three years old, and a she goat of three years old, and a ram of three years old, and a turtledove, and a young pigeon.... And he took unto him all these, and divided them in the midst, and laid each piece one against another" (Gen. 15:9-10).

It was still the early morning. The day was young, and Abraham sat down to watch. Then there came a long pause. Hour after hour passed by, but God did not give a sign or utter a single word. Judging by appearances, there was neither voice nor any to answer nor any that regarded.

Higher and ever higher the sun drove his chariot up the sky, shining with torrid heat on those pieces of flesh lying there exposed upon the sand, but still no voice or vision came. The vultures, attracted by the scent of carrion, drew together as to a feast and demanded incessant attention if they were to be kept away. Did Abraham ever permit himself to imagine that he was sitting there on a fool's mission? Did not the thought instill itself into his mind that perhaps he had been led to arrange those pieces by a freak of his own fancy and that God would not come at all? Did he shrink from the curious gaze of his servants and of Sarah his wife because he was half-conscious of having taken up a position he could not justify?

We cannot tell what passed through the heavily tried heart of Abraham during those long hours. But this, at least, we recognize: this is in a line with the discipline through which we all have to pass. Hours of waiting for God! Days of watching! Nights of sleepless vigil! Looking for the remote outposts of the relief that tarries! Wondering why the Master comes not! Climbing the hill again and again, to return without the expected vision! Watching for some long-expected letter until the path to the post office is trodden down with constant passing to and fro and wet with many tears! But all in vain! Ay, but it is not in vain. For these long waiting hours are building up the fabric of the spirit life—with gold and silver and precious stones—so as to become a thing of beauty and a joy forevermore.

Only let us see to it that we never relax our attitude of patience but wait to the end for the grace to be brought to us. And let us give the unclean birds no portion. We cannot stop them from sailing slowly through the air or uttering dismal screams or circling around us as if to pounce. But we *can* keep them from settling down. And this we must do, in the name and by the help of God. "If the vision tarry, wait for it."

THE HORROR OF A GREAT DARKNESS

The sun at last went down, and the swift eastern night cast its heavy veil over the scene. Worn out with the mental conflict, the watchings, and the labors of the day, Abraham fell into a deep sleep. And in that sleep his soul was oppressed with a dense and dreadful darkness, such as almost stifled him and lay like a nightmare upon his heart. "Lo, a horror of great darkness fell upon him" (Gen. 15:12).

Do my readers understand something of the horror of that darkness? It can occur when one who has been brought up in a traditional belief, which fails to satisfy the instincts of maturer life, supposes that in letting go of the creed there must also be the renunciation of all faith and hope, not seeing that the form may go while the essential substance may remain. It can happen when one, mistaking the nature of sin and the mercy of God, fears that there has been committed an unpardonable sin or that the bounds of repentance have been overstepped forever. For some it comes in the form of a terrible sorrow that seems so hard to reconcile with perfect love, crushing down upon the soul, wringing from it all its peaceful rest in the pitifulness of God, and launching it on a sea unlit by a ray of hope. When unkindness and cruelty and monstrous injustice harass and mock and maltreat the trusting heart, the heart begins to doubt whether there is a God overhead who can see and still permit. These people know something of the horror of total darkness and what weird and frightful visions will in that darkness pass one after another before the spirit, like the phantoms of a drunkard's delirium or the apparitions of an unhealthy brain.

It was a long and dark prospect that unfolded itself before Abraham, who beheld the history of his people through coming centuries, strangers in a foreign land, enslaved and afflicted. Did Abraham not see the anguish of their soul and their cruel bondage beneath the taskmaster's whips? Did he not hear their groans and see mothers weeping over their babes, doomed to the insatiable Nile? Did he not witness the building of pyramids and treasure-city, cemented by blood and suffering? It was, indeed, enough to fill him with darkness that could be felt.

And yet the somber woof was crossed by the warp of silver threads. The enslaved were to come out, and to come out with great substance, their oppressors being overwhelmed with crushing judgment. They were to come into that land again, while, as for himself, Abraham should go to his fathers in peace and be buried in a good old age.

It is thus that human life is made up: brightness and gloom, shadow and sun, long tracks of cloud succeeded by brilliant glints of light. And amid all, divine justice is working out its own schemes, affecting others equally with the individual soul that seems the subject of special discipline. The children of Abraham must not inherit the land of promise until the fourth generation has passed away, because the iniquity of the Amorites had not yet filled up the measure of their doom. Only then—when the reformation of that race was impossible, when their condition had become irremediable and their existence was a menace to the peace and purity of mankind—was the order given for their extermination and for the transference of their power to those who might hold it more worthily.

Oh, you who are filled with the horror of great darkness because of God's dealings with mankind, learn to trust the infallible wisdom that is an equal judge with immutable justice. Believe that He who passed through the horror of the darkness of Calvary with the cry of forsakenness is ready to bear you company through the valley of the shadow of death, till you see the sun shining upon its further side. "Who is among you that...walketh in darkness, and hath no light? let him trust in the name of the LORD, and stay upon his God" (Isa. 50:10).

THE RATIFICATION OF THE COVENANT

When Abraham awoke, the sun was down. Darkness reigned supreme. "It was dark" (Gen. 15:17). A solemn stillness brooded over the world. Then came the awful act of ratification. For the first time since man had left the gates of Eden, there appeared the symbol of the glory of God—that fearful light that was afterward to shine in the pillar of cloud and the Shekinah gleam. In the thick darkness, that mysterious light—a lamp of fire—passed slowly and majestically between the divided pieces, and as it did so, a voice said, "Unto thy seed have I given this land, from the river of Egypt unto the great river, the river Euphrates" (Gen. 15:18).

Remember that promise. It was made with the most solemn sanctions, never repealed since and never perfectly fulfilled. For a few years during the reign of Solomon, the dominion of Israel almost touched these limits, but only for a very brief period. The perfect fulfillment is yet in the future. Somehow the descendants of Abraham shall yet inherit their own land, secured to them by the covenant of God. Those rivers shall yet form their boundary lines, for "the mouth of the Lord hath spoken it" (Isa. 40:5). The entire land that awaits the Jewish people and the people that await the land may be reunited beneath the blessing of Him who by word and oath gave strong consolation to the patriarch Abraham.

As we turn from this scene—in which God bound Himself by such solemn sanctions to strengthen the ground of His servant's faith—we may carry with us exalted conceptions of His great goodness, which will humble itself so low to secure the trust of one poor heart. By two immutable things, His word and His oath, God has given strong assurance to us who are menaced by the storm, drawing us on to the rocky shore. Let us, by our divine Forerunner, drop our anchor of hope within the veil that separates us from the unseen. Here it will fasten in ground that will not yield but will hold until the eternal day dawns and we follow it into the haven guaranteed to us by God's immutable counsel (Heb. 6:19–20).

12

Hagar, the Slave Girl

Now Sarai, Abram's wife, bare him no children:
and she had a handmaid,
an Egyptian, whose name was Hagar.
Genesis 16:1

*N*one of us know all that is involved when we tear ourselves from the familiar scenes of our Harans to follow God into the lands of separation that lie beyond the river. The separated life cannot be an easy one. We may dimly guess this as we step out into the untried and unknown, but God graciously veils from our eyes that which would needlessly startle and daunt us, and He unfolds to us His requirements only as we are able to bear them.

The difficulties of the separated life arise not from any arbitrary appointments of divine providence but from the persistent manifestation of the self-life in its many alterable forms. It is absurd to say that the self-life dies once for all in some early stage of the Christian life, and it is perilous to lead men to think so. When men think or boast that it is dead, it peeps out in their very assertions and laughs at the success of its efforts to blind them to its presence. This is the masterpiece of its art: to cajole its victims into thinking that it is dead. Thieves always like to secure the insertion of a paragraph in the newspapers announcing that they have left the neighborhood, because in the false security that is generated by the announcement, they are enabled to extend their plans of pillage.

We declare, in the first moments of consecration, that we are eager not only to be reckoned dead in the sight of God as far as our self-life is concerned but also to be dead. And if we really mean what we say, God undertakes the work—first of revealing the insidious presence of the self-life where we had least expected it, and then of nailing it in bitter suffering to the cross of a painful death. You who know something of the true condition of your inner life, do not your hearts bear witness that as the light of heaven breaks with glowing glory on your souls, it reveals unexpected glimpses into the insidious workings of self? Those revelations are so clear that you are driven to claim: first, divine forgiveness for harboring such a traitor, and then, the intervention of divine grace to measure out that death, which is the only condition of growth and blessedness.

There is in this incidence a very startling manifestation of the tenacity with which Abraham's self-life still survived. We might have expected that by this time it had been extinguished. There was the long waiting of ten slow-moving years, the repeated promises of God, the practice of communion with God Himself—all this had surely been enough to eradicate and burn out all confidence in the flesh, all trust in the activities of the self-life, all desire to help himself to the realization of the promises of God. Surely, now, this proven man will wait until, in His own time and way, God shall do as He has said. Abraham would not take a shoelatchet or a thread from the King of Sodom, because he was so sure that God would *give* him all the land. Nor was he disappointed when God said, "I am thy exceeding great reward." And similarly, we might have expected that he would have strenuously resisted every attempt to persuade him to realize for himself God's promise about his seed. Surely he will wait meekly and quietly for God to fulfill His own word by the means best known to Himself.

Instead of this he listened to *the reasoning of propriety* that happened to chime in with his own thoughts, seeking to gratify the promptings of his spirit by doing something to secure the result of which God had spoken. Simple-hearted faith waits for God to unfold His purpose, sure that He will not fail. But mistrust, reacting on the self-life, leads us to take matters into our own hands—as Saul did when he took upon himself to offer sacrifice without awaiting the arrival of Samuel (1 Sam. 13).

THE SOURCE OF THESE REASONINGS

"Sarai said unto Abram" (Gen. 16:2). Poor Sarah! She had not had her husband's advantages. When he had been standing in fellowship with God, she had been quietly pursuing the routine of household duty, pondering many things.

It was clear that Abraham should have a son, but it was not definitely said by God that the child would be hers. Abraham was a strict monogamist, but the laxer notions of those days warranted the filling of the harem with others, who occupied an inferior rank to that of the principal wife, and whose children, according to common practice, were reckoned as if they were her own. Why should her husband not fall in with those laxer notions of the marriage vow? Why should he not marry the slave girl, whom they had either purchased in an Egyptian slave market or acquired among the other gifts with which Pharaoh had sent them away?

It was an heroic sacrifice for Sarah to make. She was willing to forego a woman's dearest prerogative, to put another in her own place, and to surrender a position to which she had a perfect right to cling, even though it seemed to clash with the direct promise of God. But her love for Abraham, her despair of having a child of her own, and her inability to imagine that God would fulfill His word by other than natural means—all these things combined to make the proposal from which, in another aspect, her nature as his wife must have shrunk. Love in Sarah did violence to love.

No one else could have approached Abraham with such a proposition with the slightest hope of success. But when Sarah made it, the case was altered. The suggestion might have crossed his own mind in his weaker moments, only to be instantly rejected and put aside as doing a grievous wrong to his faithful wife. But now, as it had come from her, there seemed less fear of it. It was supported by the susceptibilities of natural instinct. It was consistent with the whisperings of doubt. It seemed to be a likely means for realizing God's promise. And without hesitation or reference to

God, he fell in with the proposal. "Abram hearkened to the voice of Sarai" (Gen. 16:2).

It is always hard to resist temptation when it appeals to our natural instinct or to distrusting fear. At such an hour, if the Savior is not our Keeper, there is small hope of our being able to resist the double assault. But the temptation is still more perilous when it is presented, not by some disgusting fiend, but by some object of our love—someone who, like Sarah, has been the partner of our pilgrimage and who is willing to sacrifice all to obtain a blessing that God has promised but has not yet bestowed.

We should be exceedingly careful before acting on the suggestions of any who are not as advanced as we are in the divine life. What may seem right to them may be terribly wrong for us. And we should be especially careful to scrutinize and weigh any proposals that harmonize completely with the tendencies of our self-life. "If...the wife of thy bosom, or thy friend, which is as thine own soul, entice thee secretly...Thou shalt not consent unto him, nor hearken unto him; neither shall thine eye pity him, neither shalt thou spare" (Deut. 13:6, 8). But does not the response of the soul to such suggestions indicate how far the self-life is from being dead?

THE SORROWS TO WHICH THEY LED

As soon as the object was obtained, the results, like a crop of nettles, began to appear in that home, which had been the abode of purity and bliss. It was now destined to be the scene of discord. Raised into a position of rivalry with Sarah, and expectant of giving the long desired son to Abraham and a young master to the camp, Hagar despised her childless mistress and took no pains to conceal her contempt.

This was more than Sarah could endure. It was easier to make one heroic act of self-sacrifice than to daily bear the insolent demeanor of the maid whom she had herself exalted to this position. Nor was she reasonable in her irritation. Instead of assuming the responsibility of having brought about the disturbing event that was so fraught with misery to herself, Sarah passionately upbraided her husband, saying: "My wrong be upon thee:...the LORD judge between me and thee" (Gen. 16:5).

How true this is to human nature! We take one false step, unsanctioned by God, and when we begin to discover our mistake, we give way to outbursts of wounded pride. But instead of blaming ourselves, we turn upon others, whom we may have instigated to take the wrong course, and we bitterly reproach them for wrongs of which they at most were only instruments, while we were the final cause.

Out of this fleshly contrivance sprang many sorrows. Sorrow to Sarah, who on this occasion, as afterward, must have drunk to the dregs the cup of bitter gall—of jealousy and wounded pride, of the hate and malice that always destroy peace and joy in the nature from which they stream as the fiery lava torrents from a volcanic crater. Sorrow to Hagar, driven forth as an exile from the home of which she had dreamed to become the mistress and to which she had thought herself essential. Ah, bitter disappointment! Sorrow to Abraham, loath to part with one who, to all human appearance, would now become the mother of the child who should bless his life: stung, moreover, as he was, by the unusual bitterness of his wife's reproaches.

If anyone should read these words who is tempted to use any means of human devising for the attainment of certain goals, which in themselves may be quite legitimate, let them stand still and take to heart the teachings of this narrative. For as surely as God reigns, shall every selfish means involve us in unutterable and heartrending sorrow. "From [this time] thou shalt have wars" (2 Chron. 16:9).

THE VICTIM WHOSE LIFE WAS SO LARGELY INVOLVED

We cannot be surprised at the insolent bearing of the untutored slave girl. It was only what might have been expected. But we mourn to see in her only one of the myriads who have been sacrificed to the whim or passion, to the expediency or selfishness, of men. Innocent and lighthearted, she might have been the devoted wife of some man in her own position and the mother of a happy family. But taken as she was from her true position and put into one in which she was a mother without being a lawful wife, what could her circumstance be except miserable in the home in which she had no proper status. And in the end, she would be exiled and homeless, the wanderings to which Sarah's bitter jealousy twice drove her: once for a time—afterward forever.

Abraham, for the sake of the peace of his home, dared not intervene between his wife and her slave. "Behold," said he, "thy maid is in thy hand; do to her as it pleaseth thee" (Gen. 16:6). Not slow to act upon this implied consent, the irate mistress dealt so bitterly with the girl that she fled from Sarah's face, taking to the road that was trodden by the caravans toward her native land.

"The angel of the LORD" (and here, for the first time, that significant expression is used, which is held by many to express some evident manifestation of the Son of God in angel form) "found her by a fountain of water" (Gen. 16:7), which was familiarly known in the days of Moses. Worn and weary and lonely, there she sat down to rest. How often does the angel of the Lord still find us in our extremity!—when we are running away from the place that was assigned to us, when we are evading the cross. And what questions could be more pertinent, whether to Hagar or to us: "Whence camest thou? and whither wilt thou go?" (Gen. 16:8). Reader, answer those two questions before you read further. What is your origin? and What is your destiny?

Then there followed the distinct command that applies to us evermore: "Return...and submit" (Gen. 16:9). The day would come when God Himself would open the door and send Hagar out of that house (Gen. 21:12–14). But until that moment should come, after thirteen years had rolled away, she must return to the place that she had left, bearing her burden and fulfilling her duty as best she might. "Return...and submit."

We are all prone to act as Hagar did. If our lot is hard and our cross is heavy, we start off in a fit of impatience and wounded pride. We shirk the discipline; we evade the yoke; we make our own way out of the difficulty. Ah, we shall never get right with God this way! Never! We must retrace our steps and meekly bend our necks under the yoke. We must accept the lot that God has ordained for us, even though it may be the result of the cruelty and sin of others. We shall conquer by yielding. We shall escape by returning. We shall become free by offering ourselves to be bound. "Return...and submit." By and by, when the lesson is perfectly learned, the prison door will open of its own accord.

Meanwhile, the heart of the prodigal is cheered by promise (Gen. 16:10). The angel of the Lord unfolds all the blessed results of obedience. And as the spirit considers these, it finds the homeward way no longer lined by sharp rocks but soft with flowers.

Nor is this all. In addition to promise, there breaks on the soul the conception of One who lives and sees, who lives to avenge the wronged and to defend the helpless, and who sees each tear and pang of the afflicted soul.

"Thou God seeth me" (Gen. 16:13). Not like those blind Egyptian idols that stare with stony gaze across the desert, having eyes, though they see not. It was a new thought to the untutored slave girl, but it is familiar enough to us. And yet we might find new depths of meaning in life and duty if every moment were spent in the continual realization of these words. Let us look to Him who sees us. Let us often stop the whir of life's noise to say softly to ourselves, "God is here; God is near; God sees—He will provide; He will defend; He will avenge." "For the eyes of the LORD run to and fro throughout the whole earth, to shew himself strong in the behalf of them whose heart is perfect toward him" (2 Chron. 16:9; Zech. 4:10).

13

"Be Thou Perfect!"

I am the Almighty God;
walk before me, and be thou perfect.
Genesis 17:1

*T*hirteen long years passed slowly on after the return of Hagar to Abraham's camp. The child Ishmael was born and grew up in the patriarch's house—the acknowledged heir of the camp and yet showing symptoms of the wildness of which the angel had spoken (Gen. 16:12). Abraham may have been troubled with those strange manifestations, and yet the heart of the old man warmed to the lad and clung to him, often asking that Ishmael might live before God.

And throughout that long period there was no fresh appearance, no new announcement. Never since God had spoken to him in Charran had there been so long a pause. And it must have been a terrible ordeal, driving him back on the promise that had been given and searching his heart to determine whether the cause lay within himself. Such silences have always exercised the hearts of God's saints, leading them to say with the psalmist: "Be not silent to me: lest, if thou be silent to me, I become like them that go down into the pit" (Ps. 28:1). And yet those times are to the heart what the long silence of winter is to the world of nature in preparing it for the outburst of spring.

Some people are always on the lookout for divine appearances, for special manifestations, for celestial voices. If these are withheld, they are almost ready to break their hearts. And their life tends to an incessant straining after some startling evidence of the nearness and the love of God. This passion is unwholesome and mistaken. Such manifestations are indeed delightful, but they are meant as the bright surprises and not as the rule of Christian life. They grace our lives as a holiday breaks the school routine of a child, awakening the thrilling and unexpected emotions of joy. It is true that they are likely to be withheld when we are walking at a distance from God or indulging in coldheartedness and sin. But it is not always so. And when the child of God has lost these bright visitations for long and sad intervals—if, so far as can be determined, there is no sense of condemnation on the heart for real sin—it must be believed that they are withheld to test the inner life and to teach the necessity of basing it on faith alone rather than on feelings—no matter how good—or experience—however divine.

At last, "when Abram was ninety years old and nine," the Lord appeared to him again and gave him a new revelation of Himself. To Abraham the terms of His covenant were revealed, and Abraham was given the memorable charge that rings its summons in the ear and heart of every believer still: "Walk before me, and be thou perfect."

THE DIVINE SUMMONS

"Walk before me, and be thou perfect." Men have sadly stumbled over that word. They have not erred when they have taught that there is an experience of holiness denoted by the phrase that is possible to men. But they have sadly erred in pressing their own significance into the word, asserting that men are expected to fulfill it or that they have attained it personally.

"Perfection" is often supposed to denote sinlessness of moral character, which at the best is only a negative conception and fails to bring out the positive force of this mighty word. Surely perfection means more than sinlessness. And if this is admitted and the further admission is made that it contains the thought of moral complete-ness, it becomes yet more absurd for any mortal to assert it of himself. The very assertion shows the lack of any such thing, reveal-ing but slender knowledge of the inner life and of the nature of sin.

Absolute sinlessness is surely impossible for us as long as we do not have perfect knowledge. We know that as our moral light is growing constantly, we are constantly discovering evil in things that we once allowed without shame. If those who assert their sinless-ness live but a few years longer and continue to grow, they will be compelled to admit, if they are true to themselves, that there was evil in things that they now deem to be harmless. But whether they admit it or not, their shortcomings are not less sinful in the sight of the holy God, although undetected by their own fallible judgment.

And as to *moral completeness*, it is enough to compare the best man whom we ever knew with the perfect beauty of God incarnate to feel how monstrous such an assumption is. Surely the language of the apostle Paul is more fitting upon our lips, as he cries, "Not as though I had already attained, either were already perfect: but I fol-low after" (Phil. 3:12). Perhaps in the timeless noon of eternity such words will still best suit our lips.

Besides all this, the word *perfect* carries very different render-ings from those often given to it. For instance, when we are told that the man of God may be *perfect* (2 Tim. 3:17), the underlying thought, as any Greek scholar would affirm, is that of a workman being "thoroughly equipped for his work," as when a carpenter comes to the house, bearing in his hand the bag in which all nec-essary tools are readily available. Again, when we join in the prayer that the "God of peace...make you *perfect* in every good work to do his will," we are, in fact, asking that we may be "put in joint" with the blessed Lord, so that the glorious Head may freely secure through us the doing of His will (Heb. 13:20–21). Again, when our Lord bids us be *perfect* as our Father in heaven is perfect (Matt. 5:48), He simply prompts us to that "impartiality of mercy" that knows no distinctions of evil and good, of unjust and just, but dis-tributes its favors with bountiful and equal hand.

What, then, is the true force and significance of this word in that stirring command that lies before us here, "Walk before me, and be thou perfect?" A comparison of the various passages where it occurs establishes its meaning beyond a doubt, compelling us to read into it the thought of "wholeheartedness." The word denotes the entire surrender of the being and may be fairly expressed in the well-known words of the sweet and gifted songwriter: *Truehearted, wholehearted, faithful and loyal, King of our lives, by Thy grace will we be.*

This quality of wholehearted devotion has ever been dear to God. It was this that He considered in Job and loved in David. It is in favor of this that His eyes run to and fro to show Himself strong (2 Chron. 16:9). It is for this that He pleads with Abraham, and it was because He met with it to so large an extent in Abraham's character and obedience that He entered into eternal covenant bond with him and his descendants.

Here may the reader turn from the printed page to the record of the inner life lying open to God alone. It is right to ask, "Is my heart perfect with God? Am I wholehearted toward Him? Is He first in my plans, pleasures, friendships, thoughts, and actions? Is His will my law, His love my light, His business my aim, His 'well-done!' my exceeding great reward? Do others share me with Him?"

There is no life to be compared with that of which the undivided heart is the center and spring. Why not seek it now? Turn to God in holy contemplation and ask Him to bring your whole inner realm under His government and to hold it as His forevermore. "If therefore thine eye be single, thy whole body shall be full of light" (Matt. 6:22).

Such an attitude can be *maintained only by a very careful walk.* "Walk before me, and be thou perfect." We must seek to realize constantly the presence of God, becoming instantly aware when the whitest cloud draws its veil for a moment over His face and asking whether the cause may not lie in some barely noticed sin. We must cultivate the habit of feeling Him near, as the Friend from whom we would never be separated—in work, in prayer, in recreation, in rest. We must guard against the restlessness and unrestraint, the excessive eagerness and impatience that drown the accents of His still, small voice. We must renounce all the means that He does not inspire, all actions He does not promote. We must often turn from the friend, the poem, the landscape, or the task to look up into His face with a smile of loving recognition. We must constantly have our hearts synchronized to His eternal movements.

All this must be, and yet we shall not live forced or unnatural lives. No one will be as cheerful or lighthearted as we are. As a shining moon circles around its planet because the planet obeys the law of gravitation to the sun, so the circles of our daily life will move on in unbroken order and beauty. Would you walk before God? Then let there be nothing in heart or life that you would not open to the inspection of His holy and caring eye.

THE REVELATION ON WHICH THIS SUMMONS WAS BASED

"I am the Almighty God" ("EL-SHADDAI"). What a name is this! And what powerful emotions it must have excited in the rapt heart of the listener! God had been known to Abraham by other names, but not by this. And this was the first of a series of revelations of those depths of meaning that lay in the fathomless abyss of the divine name, each disclosure marking an epoch in the history of the race.

In God's dealings with men you will invariably find that some transcendent revelation precedes the divine summons to new and difficult duty. Promise opens the door to precept. God gives what He commands before He commands what He wills. And on this principle God acted here. It was no child's play to which He called His servant. To walk always before Him, even when the heart was weak, strength was frail, and the temptation strong to swerve to the right or left. To be perfect in devotion and obedience, when so many crosslights distracted and perplexed and fascinated the soul. To forego all methods of self-help, however tempting. To be separated from all alliances that others permitted or followed. This was much.

It was possible only through the power of the Almighty. Abraham could do all these things only on the condition—which the apostle insisted in later days—that God should strengthen him. And therefore it was necessary that the assurance be given to Abraham: "I am the Almighty God." It is as if He had said: "All power is Mine in heaven and upon earth. Of old I laid the foundations of the earth, and the heavens are the work of My hands. I sit upon the circle of the earth, and its inhabitants are as grasshoppers. I bring out the starry hosts by number, calling them all by names, by the greatness of My might, for I am strong in power. Have you not known, have you not heard, that the everlasting God, the Lord, the Creator of the ends of the earth fainteth not, neither is weary?"

All this is as true today as ever. And if any will dare venture forth on the path of separation, cutting themselves apart from all creature aid and from all self-originated effort, content to walk alone with God with no help from any but Him—such will find that all the resources of the divine Almightiness will be placed at their disposal and that the resources of omnipotence must be exhausted before their cause can fail from a lack of help. O children of God, why do we run to and fro for the help of man, when the power of God is within reach of the perfect heart? But this condition must be fulfilled before that mighty power can be put in operation on our behalf. "To him that overcometh will I give...a white stone, and in the stone a new name written" (Rev. 2:17). In Abraham's case, that name, graved on the glistening jewel, was "I am the Almighty God;" for Moses it was "Jehovah;" for us it is "the God and Father of our Lord Jesus Christ."

THE COVENANT THAT WAS DIVINELY PROPOSED

"And I will make my covenant between me and thee" (Gen. 17:2). A covenant is a promise made under the most solemn sanctions, binding the consenting parties in the most definite and impressive way. What mortal would not consent when the Almighty God proposed to enter into an everlasting covenant with His creature, ordered in all things, and sure and more stable than the everlasting hills!

It referred to the seed. This time, note the marked advance. In Haran it ran: "I will make of thee a great nation." At Bethel: "Thy seed shall be as the dust of the earth." At Mamre: "Tell the stars; so shall thy seed be." But now, three times over, the patriarch is told that he should be the father of many nations, a phrase explained by the apostle as including all peoples who share Abraham's faith, though not necessarily born from him in the line of natural descent (Gal. 3:7–29). In memory of that promise, his name was slighty altered, so that it signified the "father of a great multitude." "Nations of thee, and kings shall come of thee" (Gen. 17:6). We are included in the golden circle of those words, if we believe; and we may claim the spiritual part, at least, of this covenant that was made with Abraham before he was circumcised.

It referred to the land. "And I will give unto thee, and to thy seed after thee, the land wherein thou art a stranger, all the land of

Canaan, for an everlasting possession" (Gen. 17:8). This promise waits for fulfillment. The word *everlasting* must mean something more than those few centuries of broken, erratic rule. There is a time coming, no doubt, when our covenant-keeping God will build again the tabernacle of David, which has fallen down, and will repair the ruins thereof; and the land that now sighs shall be again inhabited by the seed of Abraham His friend.

It referred to the coming child. Until then, Abraham had no other thought than that Ishmael should be his heir. But this could not be (1) because Ishmael was born of a slave, and the slave does abide in the house forever, and (2) because he was a child of the flesh and not the direct gift of God. Abraham had been left to wait till all hope of children had become as remote to him as it had been for years for his wife. It appeared that the heir should evidently be the creation of the Almighty God, whose name was disclosed before this astounding announcement was made. This is why we are kept waiting till all human and natural hope has died from our hearts, so that God may be All in all. "And God said, Sarah thy wife shall bear thee a son indeed; and thou shalt call his name Isaac" (Gen. 17:19).

For us there is yet a crowning sweetness in the words "I will be a God unto thee, and to thy seed," words repeated in Hebrews 8:10, so as certainly to include us all, if we believe. Who can unfold all the wealth of meaning of these words? All light, and no darkness at all. All love, and no shadow of change. All strength, and no sign of weakness. Beauty, sweetness, glory, majesty—all are in God, and all these will be ours if God says to us, "I will be a God unto thee."

Nor shall this heritage be ours only. It shall belong to our children also if we exercise Abraham's faith. God pledges Himself to be the God of our seed. But it is for us to claim the fulfillment of His pledge. Not in heartrending cries but in quiet, determined faith, let us ask Him to do as He has said.

14

THE SIGN OF
THE COVENANT

And I will make my covenant between me and thee,
and will multiply thee exceedingly.

Genesis 17:2

*T*hree times over in Scripture, Abraham is called "the friend of God." In that moment of agony, when tidings came to King Jehoshaphat of the great heathen alliance that had been formed against him, he stood in the temple and said, "Art not thou our God, who didst drive out the inhabitants of this land...and gavest it to the seed of Abraham thy friend for ever?" (2 Chron. 20:7).

And the apostle James, at the close of his argument about faith and works, tells us that when Abraham believed God, "it was imputed unto him for righteousness: and he was called the Friend of God" (James 2:23).

But better than all, Jehovah Himself uses the title of friendship and acknowledges the sacred tie between this much tried spirit and Himself: "But thou, Israel, art my servant, Jacob whom I have chosen, the seed of Abraham my friend" (Isa. 41:8).

And it would almost appear that these two chapters, Genesis 17 and 18, were written for this reason: to show the familiarity and intimacy that existed between the Eternal God and the man who was honored to be called His friend. However, in reading them, we must not suppose that there was something altogether exceptional and unique in this marvelous story. Without doubt it is a true record of what happened more than three thousand years ago, but it is surely also intended as an example of the way in which the Eternal God is willing to deal with truehearted saints in all ages. To hundreds and thousands of His saints, God has been all that He was to Abraham, and He is willing to be all that to us still.

Let us examine these ancient lines beneath the flood of light shed on them by our Savior when He said: "Henceforth I call you not servants; for the servant knoweth not what his lord doeth: but I have called you friends" (John 15:15).

The friendship of God is freely offered to us in Jesus Christ our Lord. We cannot merit or deserve it. We cannot establish a prior claim to it. We are simply His bankrupt debtors forever, wondering at the heights and depths, the lengths and breadths of the unsearchable riches of His grace. May we not say that one ultimate cause of this friendship is in the yearning of the heart of the Eternal for fellowship? But it must remain forever a mystery why He should seek it among us—the fallen children of Adam, the tenants of bodies of dust, the ants on the tiny leaf, called Earth, amid the forest foliage of the universe.

We are prone to think that if He had so desired it, He might have found—or if He could not have found, He might have created—a race more noble, more obedient, more sympathetic than ours. Or at least He might have secured one that would not cost Him so dearly, demanding of Him the anguish of Gethsemane and the blood of the cross. And yet it could not be. That which is, and has been, must on the whole be the best that could be, since infinite love and wisdom have so ordered it. And perhaps none could be so perfectly the companions of the Son of God through all the ages as those who know the light because they have dwelt in the darkness, who know the truth because they have been ensnared in the meshes of the false, and who can appreciate love because they have been in the far country, wasting their substance in riotous living, but have been redeemed by His blood.

What a wondrous destiny there is within our reach! One to which the angels might aspire in vain! At the best they can only be ministers, flames of fire, hearts of love, excelling in strength, hearkening to His word. But we may be the friends of God, sons and daughters of the great King, members of the body of Christ, constituent parts of His Bride, in her peerless beauty and readiness for her Spouse. As one writes such words as these, the brain almost reels beneath the conception that flashes before it of the blessedness that awaits us, both in this world and in those ages that rear their heads in the far distance, as lines on lines of snowy breakers rolling in from a sunlit sea.

O friends of God, why do you not make more of your transcendent privileges? Why do you not talk to Him about all that wearies and worries you as freely as Abraham did, telling Him about your Ishmaels, your Lots, and His dealings? Why do you not fall on your face while God talks with you (Gen. 17:3)? Life should be one long conversation between God and us. No day should ever close without our talking over its history with our patient and loving Lord, entering into His confessional, relieving our hearts of half their sorrow, and all their bitterness, in the act of telling Him all. And if only we get low enough and are still enough, we shall hear His accents sweet and thrilling, soft and low, opening depths that no eye has seen nor ear heard, but which He has prepared for those who love and wait for Him.

There are, however, three conditions that we must fulfill if we would enjoy this blessed friendship: *separation*, *purity*, and *obedience*. Each condition was set forth in the rite of circumcision, which was given to Abraham for himself and his descendants at this time.

Circumcision seems to have been in vogue among the Egyptians and other nations even before it was taken up and adopted as the seal of the sacred covenant between God and Abraham. It existed previously, but it had never borne the interpretation with which it was now invested through Abraham. The same was true of how the immersion of new disciples had been long practiced by both John the Baptist and the Jews before our Lord appropriated it and gave it a significance that opened up an entirely fresh depth of meaning and beauty.

All of us are more or less dependent on outward symbols and signs, and Abraham and his children were no exception to this rule.

Therefore, it seemed good to God to carve in the flesh of His people an unmistakable reminder and sacrament of that holy relationship into which they had entered. A similar function in the Christian Church is met by the ordinances of baptism and the Lord's Supper.

The rite of circumcision was rigorously maintained among the children of Abraham. Moses was not permitted to undertake his life-work while his son was left uncircumcised. Nor were the people allowed to enter Canaan until they had rolled away the reproach of Canaan and had submitted to this rite on the threshold of the land of promise. The sanctity of the Sabbath might at any time be invaded rather than permit the eighth day of a child's life to pass without the act of circumcision being performed. It is said of the child Jesus that "eight days were accomplished for the circumcising of the child" (Luke 2:21). Paul noted the fact that in his own life, according to Jewish usage, he was "circumcised the eighth day" (Phil. 3:5). And no one could receive benefit through the sin offering or sacrifice who had not passed through this initiatory rite. So strict was the line of demarcation that the Jew counted the uncircumcised as unclean and would not eat with them or go into their houses. It was a formidable charge against the apostle Peter on his return to Jerusalem from visiting in the house of Cornelius, "Thou wentest in to men uncircumcised, and didst eat with them" (Acts 11:3).

It was concerning this matter that a major controversy began in the early Church. The Pharisee party was quite willing for Gentiles to meet with them in Church fellowship, but only if they were circumcised as Jews. They went so far as to affirm, "Except ye be circumcised after the manner of Moses, ye cannot be saved" (Acts 15:1, 24). And, not content with affirming this in Antioch and Jerusalem, they sent their emissaries far and wide, especially visiting the infant churches that had been recently founded by the apostle Paul's painstaking care and insisting upon the circumcision of the new converts.

There was no compromise possible in this matter. Both the Council at Jerusalem (Acts 15) and the apostle Paul, guided by the Spirit of God, made it abundantly clear, both by circular letter and by epistle, that circumcision was part of the temporary ritual of Judaism that was destined to pass away. "If ye be circumcised, Christ shall profit you nothing.... [In the new man] there is neither...

circumcision nor uncircumcision.... For in Christ Jesus neither circumcision availeth any thing, nor uncircumcision, but a new
creature" (Gal. 5:2; Col. 3:11; Gal. 6:15). And thus this danger of the
Church becoming a Jewish institution—a kind of inner circle of the
Judaistic commonwealth—was averted, and the Church maintained
itself as the common meeting ground for all who loved, trusted, and
obeyed the Lord Jesus in sincerity.

At the same time, as in so many other Jewish rites, there was an
inner spirit that passed on into the Christian Church and is our heritage today. St. Paul, the deadly foe of the outward rite as a means
of salvation, speaks of a spiritual circumcision that is made without
human hands by the direct introduction of the Holy Spirit. It consists
of "putting off the body of the sins of the flesh" (Col. 2:11). O
blessed High Priest, this is what we need: take the knife in hand
and, though it cost us blood, make haste to set us free from the
dominion of evil and to constitute us the true circumcision: "For we
are the circumcision, which worship God in the spirit, and rejoice in
Christ Jesus, and have no confidence in the flesh" (Phil. 3:3).

It is only in proportion as we know the spiritual meaning of circumcision that we can enter into the joyous granting of the
friendship of God. But if we are willing, our Lord and Savior is both
able and willing to effect in us this blessed spiritual result.

SEPARATION

Through circumcision, Abraham and his seed were marked out
as a separated people. And it is only as such that any of us can be
admitted into the friendship of God. The shedding of blood and
death—the cross and the grave—must lie between us and our own
past life; yes, between us and all participation with evil. The only
appointed place for Christ and His followers is outside the camp,
where the ground is still freshly trodden by the feet of the exiled
King.

There are times when we may be specifically shown to abide
where we were originally called of God. But this will be for special
purposes of ministry, because the darkness needs light. For the most
part, the clarion note rings out to all who desire to know the delights
of divine fellowship: "Wherefore come out from among them, and
be ye separate, saith the Lord, and touch not the unclean thing; and
I will receive you, and will be a Father unto you" (2 Cor. 6:17–18).

This was the key to Abraham's life, and it is the inner meaning of the rite of circumcision.

PURITY

"Putting off the body of the sins of the flesh by the circumcision of Christ" (Col. 2:11). There is hardly a single grace dearer to God than this—for the believer to keep lily-white amid the defiling atmosphere, to walk with unspotted garments even in Sardis, to be as sensitive to the taint of impurity as the most delicate nostril is to an evil odor. Ah, this is a condition of great price in the sight of God, and one to which He unveils Himself! "Blessed are the pure in heart: for they shall see God" (Matt. 5:8).

Purity can be attained only by the special grace of the Holy Spirit and by doing two things: first, by our turning away from anything that we know leads us into sinful thoughts and impure imaginations; second, by our seeking immediate forgiveness when we are conscious of having yielded, even for a moment, to the deadly and insidious fascinations of the flesh.

There are some who yearn for the white rose of chastity with a kind of despair that it should ever become their own. They forget that it is possible to us only by the grace of Christ and through the Holy Spirit, whose temples we profess ourselves to be. Let us trust Him to keep His own possessions in the perfect loveliness of that purity and chastity that are so dear to God; this is the circumcision of Christ.

OBEDIENCE

For Abraham, this rite might have seemed less necessary than for some in his camp. But no sooner was it commanded than it was undergone. "In the selfsame day was Abraham circumcised, and Ishmael his son" (Gen. 17:26). Does it not remind us of Him who said, "Ye are my friends, if ye do whatsoever I command you" (John 15:14)? Instant obedience to known duty is an indispensable condition of all intimacy with God. If the duty is distressing and difficult, remember to claim all the more of the divine grace. We need to know that there is no duty to which we are called for which there is not strength enough within reach to accomplish it if only we will put forth our hands to take it.

We do not obey to become friends, but having become friends, we hasten to obey. Love is more uncompromising than law. And for the love of Him who calls us by so dear a title we are glad to undertake and accomplish what Sinai with all its thunders would fail to strengthen us to attempt.

Of the secrets that shall be revealed, of the delights that shall be experienced, and of the blessings that shall gather to ever widening circles through the friendship of one man with God, we do not have space to write. This, however, is true, that the soul laughs to itself (Gen. 17:17), not with disbelief but with the uncontrollable gladness of conscious acceptance and love.

15

THE DIVINE GUEST

And the LORD appeared unto [Abraham]
in the plains of Mamre.

Genesis 18:1

*W*hen, in the course of some royal passage, a king condescends to stop in the home of one of the subjects of his realm, the event immediately becomes the theme of chroniclers, and the family selected for so high an honor is held in deepened respect. But what shall we say in the presence of such an episode as this—where the God of heaven became the guest of His servant Abraham!

There is no doubt as to the glorious character of one of the three who visited the tent of the patriarch on that memorable afternoon, when every living thing was seeking shelter during the heat of the day. In the first verse we are expressly told that Jehovah appeared to Abraham as he sat in the tent door in the heat of the day. And in the tenth verse there is the intonation of deity, who alone can create life and to whom nothing is too hard, in the words of promise that tell with unmistakable certainty that Sarah would have a son. And, besides, we are told that two angels came to Sodom at evening. Evidently they were two of the three who had sat as Abraham's guests beneath the tree that sheltered his tent in the blazing noon. But as for the other, who throughout the wondrous hours had been the only spokesman, His dignity is disclosed in the amazing colloquy that took place on the heights of Mamre, when Abraham stood yet before the Lord and pleaded with Him as the Judge of all the earth.

It was in this manner that the Son of God anticipated His incarnation and was found in fashion as a man before He became flesh. He loved to come *incognito* into the homes of those He cherished as His friends, even before He came across the slopes of Olivet to make His home in the favored cottage of Lazarus, where His spirit rested from the clamor of the great city and prepared Himself for the cross and the tomb. "Rejoicing in the habitable part of his earth; and my delights were with the sons of men" (Prov. 8:31).

It is very marvelous! We may well ask with deepest reverence and awe the question of Solomon when he felt the utter inadequacy of his splendid temple as the abode of the Eternal God: "But will God indeed dwell on the earth? behold, the heaven and heaven of heavens cannot contain thee; how much less this house that I have builded?" (1 Kings 8:27). But this question has been forever settled by God Himself in the majestic words: "For thus saith the high and lofty One that inhabiteth eternity, whose name is Holy; I dwell in the high and holy place, with him also that is of a contrite and humble spirit, to revive the spirit of the humble, and to revive the heart of the contrite ones" (Isa. 57:15). And the life of our blessed Master is a delightful commentary on these mighty affirmations. He said to a tax collector, "Zaccheus, make haste, and come down; for today I must abide at thy house" (Luke 19:5). He went to the home of Peter and was ministered to by one of the household whom He had raised from the gates of death. And after His resurrection, He entered the humble lodging of the two disciples in whose company He had walked from Jerusalem, seeking to dry their tears as they went.

Nor is this all. There is no heart so lowly but that He will enter. There is no home so humble but that He will make Himself a welcome guest. There is no table so poorly provisioned but that He will not join, turning water into wine, multiplying the loaves and fishes, and converting the simple meal into a sacrament. When seated at a meal with those He loves, He still takes bread and blesses it and breaks it and gives it to them (Luke 24:30). To every person He says, "Behold, I stand at the door, and knock: if any man hear my voice, and open the door, I will come in to him, and will sup with him; and he with me" (Rev. 3:20).

At the beginning, Abraham evidently did not realize the full meaning of the episode in which he was taking part. Even so do we often fail to value correctly the characters with whom we come in contact. It is only as they pass away from us forever and we look back upon them that we realize that we have been entertaining angels unawares. Let us so act always and everywhere in such a manner that we may have nothing to regret as we review the past. May we not have to criticize ourselves for having omitted to do something that we would have inserted in our program had we only realized our opportunities.

ABRAHAM TREATED HIS VISITORS WITH GREAT HOSPITALITY

In Genesis 18 we find that Abraham *ran* to meet them, bowing himself toward the ground. He offered water for their feet and rest for their tired bodies beneath the spreading shadow. He started his wife to the immediate kneading of the meal for baking on the scorching stones. He ran to choose his tenderest calf, refusing to delegate the work to another's hand. He served his visitors himself, standing as a servant by their side under the tree while they ate. Christians have not much to boast of—and a good deal to learn—as they consider the action of this elder saint and his dealings with the three strangers who came to his tent. The faith that he had toward God had a very winsome aspect toward the men. There was nothing in him that was severe or forbidding, but much that was exceedingly lovely and brimming with the milk of human kindness.

WHEN CHRIST COMES TO US IN THE FORM OF A STRANGER

Christ comes to us in the form of a stranger, but we are too busy or too tired or too afraid of making a mistake that we either refuse Him altogether or treat Him so badly that He passes unobserved away to carry to someone else the blessing that He would have left with us had we only shown ourselves worthy.

Does He not test us in this way? Of course, if He were to come in His manifested splendor as the Son of the Highest, everyone would receive Him and provide Him with lavish hospitality. But this would not reveal our true character. And so He comes to us as a wayfaring man, hungry and thirsty, or as a stranger, beggarly and sick. Those who are like Him will show Him mercy in whatever disguise He comes and will be surprised to learn that they ever ministered to Him. Those, on the other hand, who are not really His, will fail to discern Him, allowing Him to go away unhelped, and waking up to find that "inasmuch as ye did it not to one of the least of these, ye did it not to me" (Matt. 25:45).

There was an abundance of truth in the simplicity of the little German lad who left the door open for the Lord to enter and sit with his mother and himself at their frugal dinner table. This lad, when a beggar stood within the portal to ask alms, remarked: "Perhaps the Lord could not come Himself and has therefore sent this poor man as His representative."

But God Never Leaves Us in His Debt

The Lord takes care to pay for His entertainment royally and divinely. After He uses Peter's fishing boat, He gives it back, nearly submerged by the weight of the fish that He had driven into the nets. He sits down with His friends to a country marriage feast and pays for their simple fare by jars brimming with water turned to wine. He uses the five barley loaves and two small fishes, but He fills the lad with an ample meal. He sends His prophet to lodge with a widow and then provides grain and oil for him and her for many days. And Abraham was no loser by his gracious hospitality, for as they sat at the meal, the Lord foretold the birth of Sarah's child: "I will certainly return unto thee according to the time of life; and, lo, Sarah thy wife shall have a son" (Gen. 18:10).

Sarah was sitting inside the flimsy curtain of camel's hair, secluded after the Eastern fashion for those of high rank, and as she heard the words, she laughed within herself the laugh of incredulity. That laugh was at once noticed by Him from whom nothing can be hidden and whose eyes are as a flame of fire. "And the Lord said unto Abraham, Wherefore did Sarah laugh, saying, Shall I of a surety bear a child, which am old? Is any thing too hard for the Lord?" (Gen. 18:13–14).

With strange simplicity she answered through the curtain, denying that she had laughed, for she was afraid. But her reply was met by the stern and uncompromising declaration that was altogether final: "Nay; but thou didst laugh" (Gen. 18:15). These were the only audible words that we know to have passed between God and Abraham's wife, and they reveal the unbelief of her nature. But we must not judge her too harshly, for she had not had the opportunities of her husband. However, Sarah seems to have been led by these words into a true faith, for it is said, "Through faith also Sarah herself received strength to conceive seed, and was delivered of a child when she was past age, because she judged him faithful who had promised" (Heb. 11:11).

THE TRUE LAW OF FAITH

Do not look at your faith or at your feelings. Look away from yourself to the word of promise and, above all, to the Promiser. Study the preciseness of His orderings in the starry firmament. Are planets ever overdue? Do the seasons forget to revolve? Consider how accurately He has kept His word with the nations of the past, whose ruined cities attest His judgments! Has He ever failed to keep His word? Is there any conceivable reason why He should not keep it? His power is omnipotent, and would He ever have pledged Himself to do what He could not effect? "She judged him faithful who had promised" (Heb. 11:11). Look from faith to the promise, and from the promise to the Promiser. And as we become conscious of possessing the power of vision while we look on any object to which we may direct our gaze, so we shall become conscious of the presence and growth of faith as we look away to our faithful God.

"IS ANYTHING TOO HARD FOR THE LORD?"

That is one of God's unanswered questions. It has lain there for over three thousand years, studied by myriads, answered by none. Perhaps those words of Jeremiah are the only answer that mortal men can give: "Ah LORD GOD! behold, thou hast made the heaven and the earth by thy great power and stretched out arm, and there is nothing too hard for thee" (Jer. 32:17).

It may seem nearly impossible to you that God should ever keep His word in the conversion of that friend for whom you have a warrant to pray, according to 1 John 5:16. Hard to exonerate your character from the defamation with which it is being befouled. Hard to keep your evil nature in the place of death and to cast down your evil imaginings, bringing every thought into captivity to the obedience of Christ. Hard to make you sweet and gentle, forgiving and loving. Hard to produce from you the fruits of a lovely and holy nature. It may be hard, but it is not too hard for the Lord. "With God all things are possible." And, as Sarah found it, all things are possible to those who believe.

The one thing that hinders God is our unbelief. Sarah must believe, and Abraham also, before the child of promise could be born. And so it must be with us. As soon as we believe, then, according to our faith it is done to us; yes, exceeding abundantly beyond all we had asked or thought.

It may seem hard that the sins of a life should be forgiven, but God will do it for any penitent and believing soul. "All that believe [in Christ] are justified from all things" (Acts 13:39). It may seem hard that our naked souls should be clothed in robes fit for the royal palace, but it shall be so if we have faith, for the righteousness of Christ is imputed and reckoned to all who believe (Rom. 3:22). It may seem hard that rebels should become children, yet this, too, shall be, for to all who receive Him, He gives the right to become children of God (John 1:12).

You ask how to obtain this faith. Remember that faith is the receptive attitude of the soul, begotten and maintained by the grace of God. Christ is the Author and Finisher of faith, and not only in the abstract but also in the personal experience of the soul. Faith is the gift of God. If, then, you would receive it, put your will on the side of Christ. It cannot be a passing wish but must be the whole will of your being. Will to believe patiently, persistently, and yearningly. Let your eyes be ever toward the Lord; study the promises of God; consider the nature of God; be prepared to be rid of everything that grieves His Holy Spirit; and it is as certain as the truth of Christ that you will have begotten and maintained in you the faith that can move mountains and laugh at impossibilities.

And to such faith God will come, not as a passing wayfarer, but to abide, to feast with the soul in holy strengthening fellowship, to fill it with the true laughter, and to leave behind promises soon to become accomplished facts. "Behold, the tabernacle of God is with men, and he will dwell with them, and they shall be his people, and God himself shall be with them, and be their God" (Rev. 21:3).

16

PLEADING FOR SODOM

But Abraham stood yet before the LORD.
And Abraham drew near.
Genesis 18:22–23

*A*s the day wore on, Abraham's mysterious guests went off across the hills toward Sodom, and Abraham went with them to bring them on their way. But all three did not reach the guilty city, over which the thunderclouds had already commenced to gather. That evening, two angels entered it alone. And where was their companion? Ah! He had stayed behind to talk yet further with His friend Abraham. Tradition still points out the spot on the hills at the head of a long steep ravine leading down to the sullen waters of the Dead Sea, where the Lord stayed behind to tell Abraham all that was in His heart.

Why did the Lord not accompany His angels down to Sodom? Was it because vengeance is His inexplicable work, in which He can take no pleasure? It surely befits the dignity of the sovereign Judge to delegate to other hands the execution of His decrees. "The Son of man shall send forth his angels, and they shall gather out of his kingdom all things that offend, and them which do iniquity" (Matt. 13:41).

But there was a deeper reason still. Abraham was the "friend of God," and friendship constitutes a claim to be entrusted with secrets hidden from others. "The secret of the LORD is with them that fear him" (Ps. 25:14). "Henceforth," said the Master to His disciples, "I call you not servants; for the servant knoweth not what his lord doeth: but I have called you friends; for all things that I have heard of my Father I have made known unto you" (John 15:15). If we live near God, we shall have many things revealed to us that are hidden from the wise and prudent. The Septuagint version of Genesis 18:17 has well brought out the spirit of the divine musings when it puts the question this way: "Shall I hide from Abraham, *my servant*, the thing which I do?" The Lord does nothing that He does not first reveal to His holy servants and prophets.

But the words that follow point to a yet further reason for the full disclosures that were made: "For I know him, that he will command his children and his household after him, and they shall keep the way of the LORD, to do justice and judgment" (Gen. 18:19). Was there a fear lest Abraham and his children might doubt the justice of God's judgment if the righteous were summarily cut off with the wicked and if the cities of the plain were destroyed without a revelation of their sin on the one hand and the display of the divine mercy on the other? Certainly it has placed the divine character in an altogether different light, in that we have been permitted to understand some of the motives that have moved God in His goodness or severity in a case like this. And though His judgments must ever be a great deep, yet such a wondrous discourse as this shines above them as the rainbow trembles in its matchless beauty over the steamy depths of Niagara's plunge.

THE BURDEN OF THE DIVINE ANNOUNCEMENT

"The cry of Sodom and Gomorrah is great" (Gen. 18:20). What a marvelous expression! There, far down the valley, bathed in the radiance of the westering sun, lay the guilty cities, still and peaceful. No sound traveled to the patriarch's ear, not even the roar that balloonists detect in the dizzy heights of air through which they travel on their adventurous way, passing the mighty cities far beneath that betray their existence by their voice. Quiet though Sodom seemed in the far distance and in the hush of the closing day, yet to God there was a cry. The cry of the earth compelled to carry such a scar. The cry of inanimate creation, groaning and travailing in pain. The cry of the oppressed, the downtrodden, the victims of human violence and lust. The cry of the young woman, the wife, and the child. These were the cries that had entered into the ears of the Lord God of Sabaoth. And each sin has a cry. "The voice of thy brother's blood crieth unto me" (Gen. 4:10). And it will go on crying unless it is silenced by the yet greater voice of the blood of Christ "that speaketh better things than that of Abel" (Heb. 12:24). And if each sin has a cry, what is the volume of sound for a life and for a city! Must not God still have to say of our great cities, one by one—"Its cry is great; and its sin is very grievous?"

"I will go down now, and see" (Gen. 18:21). God always closely investigates the true condition of the case before He awards or executes His sentences. He comes seeking fruit for three years before He gives the order for the cutting down of the tree that drew sustenance from the vineyard soil (Luke 13:7). He walks our streets day and night. He patrols our thoroughfares, marking everything, missing nothing. He glides unasked into our most sacred privacy, for all things are naked and open to the eyes of Him with whom we have to do. He is prepared, nay, eager to give us the benefit of any excuse. But flagrant sin, like that which broke out in Sodom that very night, is enough to settle forever the fate of a Godless community when standing in the court of Him who is Judge and Witness both.

"And if not, I will know" (Gen. 18:21). There was something very ominous in all these words that Abraham clearly understood to indicate the approaching destruction of the place. Notice that in his prayer he again and again alludes to the imminence of its doom: "Wilt thou also destroy the righteous with the wicked?" (Gen. 18:23). But what is there that God does not know? "The darkness and the light are both alike to thee" (Ps. 139:12). Yet He says, "I will know." Yes, remember that from God no secrets can be hid. He will search out the most hidden ramifications of your sin, bringing them out before the gaze of the universe in a manner that justifies His righteous judgments that He will not spare.

THE IMPRESSION THAT
WAS MADE ON ABRAHAM

After the angels had gone on to Sodom, leaving Abraham alone with the Lord, Abraham was thoroughly aroused by the revelation that had broken upon him, and his mind was filled with a tumult of emotion. He hardly dared question God: what was he but "dust and ashes" (Gen. 18:27)? And yet he was driven to make some attempt to avert the doom that threatened the cities of the plain.

The motives that prompted Abraham were twofold:

(1) *There was a natural anxiety about his kinsman Lot.* Twenty years had passed since Lot had left him, but Abraham had never ceased to follow him with the most tender affection. He could not forget that Lot was the son of his dead brother Haran or that Lot had been his ward or that Lot had braved the hardships of the desert in his company. All this had been present to Abraham's mind when, a few years before, he had made a heroic effort to liberate him from the hands of Chedorlaomer. And now the strong impulse of natural affection stirred him to make one strenuous effort to save Sodom, lest his nephew might be consumed in its overthrow. True religion tends not to destroy but to fulfill all the impulses of true natural love.

(2) *There was also a fear lest the total destruction of the cities of the plain might prejudice the character of God in the minds of the neighboring peoples.* Abraham did not deny that the fate that was about to overtake them was deserved by many of the people of that wicked and luxuriant valley. But he could not bring his mind to suppose that the whole of the population was equally debased, and he feared that if all were summarily swept away, the surrounding nations would have a handle of reproach against the justice of his God. They would accuse Him of unrighteousness, inasmuch as He destroyed the righteous with the wicked.

The character of God has ever been dear to His truehearted servants of every age. Moses was prepared to forego the honor of being the ancestor of the chosen people rather than that the nations that had heard of the divine fame should be able to say that God was not able to bring them into the land of promise (Exod. 32:10; Num. 14:12). And when the men of Israel fled before Ai, Joshua and the elders appear to have thought less of the danger of an immediate rising to cut them off than of what God would do for His great name. Oh, for more of this chivalrous devotion to the interests and glory of our God! Would that we were so absorbed in all that touches the honor of the divine name among men, that this might be the supreme element in our anxiety as we view the trend of human opinion concerning the enactments of divine providence!

This passion for the glory of God burned with a clear strong flame in Abraham's heart, and it was out of this that there arose his wondrous intercession. When we become as closely identified with the interests of God as Abraham was, we shall come to feel as he did, and we shall be eager that the divine character should be vindicated among the children of men. Oh, for the contentment, to lie dying in the ditch, if need be, so long as we can hear the shouts of triumph amid which our King rides over us to victory.

THE ELEMENTS IN ABRAHAM'S INTERCESSION

It was lonely prayer. Abraham waited until on all that wide plateau and beneath those arching skies there was no living man to overhear this marvelous outpouring of a soul overcharged, as are the pools when, after the rains of spring, they overflow their banks. "Abraham stood yet before the LORD" (Gen. 18:22). Even the most intense, strongest devotion to prayer will not hold up in the presence of another person. Every saint must have a place where he can shut the door and pray to the Father who is in secret. The private place may be the mountains or the woods or the sounding shore, but it must be somewhere. Pitiable is the man who cannot—miserable the man who dare not—meet God face to face, talking with Him of His ways and pleading for his fellows.

> For what are men better than sheep or goats,
> That nourish a blind life within the brain,
> If, knowing God, they lift not hands of prayer
> Both for themselves and those who call them friend.

It was prolonged prayer. "Abraham stood yet before the LORD." The story takes but a few moments to read, but the scene may have lasted for the space of hours. We cannot climb the more elevated pinnacles of prayer in a hasty rush. They demand patience, toil, prolonged endeavor before the lower slopes can be left and the brooding cloud-line passed and the aspiring soul can reach that cleft in the mountainside, where Moses stood beneath the shadow of God's hand. Of course, our God is always on the alert to hear and answer the prayers that we fire through the busy day, but we cannot maintain this posture of brief prayer unless we cultivate the prolonged occasions. How much we miss because we do not wait before God! We do not give the sun a chance to thaw us. We do not linger long enough upon the wharf to see the great ships return freighted with the answers we had been praying for. If only we had remained longer at the palace door, we might have seen the King come out with a benediction in His face and a gift in His hands.

It was very humble prayer. "Behold now, I have taken upon me to speak unto the Lord, which am but dust and ashes" (vs. 27). "Oh let not the Lord be angry, and I will speak" (vs. 30). "Behold now, I have taken upon me to speak unto the Lord" (vs. 31). "Oh let not the Lord be angry, and I will speak yet but this once" (vs. 32). The nearer we get to God, the more conscious are we of our own unworthiness. The higher a bird flies in mid-heaven, the deeper will be the reflection of its snowy pinions in the placid lake beneath. Let the firefly compete with the meridian sun; let the dewdrop boast itself against the fullness of the ocean bed; let the babe vaunt its knowledge with the intelligence of a seraph—before the man who lives in touch with God shall think of taking any other position than that of lowliest humiliation in His presence. Before Him angels veil their faces, and the heavens are not clean in His sight. And is it not remarkable that our sense of weakness is one of our strongest claims and arguments with God? "He forgetteth not the cry of the humble" (Ps. 9:12). "To this man will I look, even to him that is poor and of a contrite spirit, and trembleth at my word" (Isa. 66:2).

This prayer was based on a belief that God possessed the same moral sentiments as Abraham himself. "Wilt thou also destroy the righteous with the wicked?... That be far from thee to do after this manner, to slay the righteous with the wicked?... Shall not the Judge of all the earth do right?" (vv. 23, 25). There is an infinite interest in this. It is as if the patriarch looked up from the clear depths of his own integrity into the azure heights of the divine being and saw there enthroned a moral nature, at least as upright, fair, and true as his own. And it was to that that he made his appeal, sure of a favorable response.

It was as if he had said: "Almighty God, I could not think it right to destroy the righteous with the wicked. And I am sure that any number of righteous men would shrink from doing so. If this is binding on man, it must be much more binding on You, because You are the Judge of all the earth." And God was not angry; indeed, He assented to Abraham's plea. And may we not go further and say that though God may act in ways above our reason, yet He will not contradict those instincts of the moral sense that He has placed within our hearts. And if at times He seems to do so, it is because we have misunderstood His dealings and put an erroneous interpretation upon them.

It was a cherished motto of bygone days that "the king could do no wrong." Alas, it was a vain dream! But what was untrue of any king is literally true of the Eternal God. He cannot outrage the moral nature in man, which is made in the likeness of His own. Let us possess our souls in patience, assured that any appearances to the contrary are the mists generated by our own evil nature or limited intelligence and that these will be swept away from obscuring that everlasting righteousness that is steadfast and changeless as the great mountains.

This prayer was persevering. Six times Abraham returned to the prayer, and as each petition was granted, his faith and courage grew. Then, finding that he had struck a right vein, he worked it again, and yet again. It looks at first sight as if he forced God back from point to point and wrenched his petitions from an unwilling hand. But this is a mistake. In point of fact, *God was drawing him on*. If Abraham had dared to ask at first what he asked at the last, he would have received more than all that he asked or thought at the very commencement of his intercession. This was the time of *his* education. Abraham did not learn the vast extent of God's righteousness and mercy all at once, but he climbed the dizzy heights step by step. As he gained each step, he was inspired to dare another. What a pity that he stopped at ten! There is no way to know what he might have reached had he gone on. As it was, the Almighty was obliged, by the demands of His own nature, to exceed the limits placed by Abraham in bringing out of Sodom the only persons that could by any possibility be accounted "righteous."

It is in this manner that God educates us still. In ever-widening circles, He tempts his new-fledged eaglets to try the sustaining buoyancy of the air. He forces us to ask one thing and then another and yet another. And when we have asked our utmost, there are always unexplored remainders behind, and He does exceeding abundantly above all. There were not ten righteous men in Sodom, but Lot and his wife and his two daughters were saved, though three of them were deeply infected with the moral contagion of the place. And God's righteousness was clearly established and vindicated in the eyes of the surrounding peoples.

In closing, we note *one of the great principles in the divine government of the world*. A whole city would have been spared if ten righteous men had been found within its walls. Ungodly men little realize how much they owe to the presence of the children of God in their midst. Long before now, the floods of deserved wrath should have swept them all away. But judgment has been restrained because God could not do anything while the righteous were found among them. The impatient servants have often asked whether they should not gather out the tares, but the answer of the righteous Lord has ever been: "Nay; lest while ye gather up the tares, ye root up also the wheat with them" (Matt. 13:29).

How little the world realizes the debt it owes to its saints—the salt to stay its corruption, the light to arrest the reinstitution of the reign of chaos and night! We cannot but yearn over the world as it rolls on its way toward its sad dark doom. Let us plead for it from the heights above Mamre. And may we and our beloved ones be led out from it into safety before the last plagues break full upon it in inevitable destruction!

17

Angel Work in a Bad Town

Genesis 19

*T*he saline waters of the Dead Sea ripple over a part of the site where once stood the cities of the plain, with their busy stir of life and thought and trade. But all the sounds of human joy, sorrow, or industry, the tread of the soldier, the call of the herdsman, the murmur of the market, the voices of little children playing in the open spaces—*all* are hushed in that awful solitude, the aspect of which is a striking testimony to the truth of the inspired Word.

Surrounded by gaunt mountains, the Dead Sea lies thirteen hundred feet below the level of the Mediterranean Sea. So strange and desolate is the scene that it was long believed that no birds would fly across the sullen waters, no shells line the beach, no trace of green vegetation is found along the shores. But strewn along the desolate edge lie trunks and branches of trees, torn from the thickets of the river jungle by the violence of the Jordan, borne rapidly into the Sea of Sodom, and cast up again from its depths, encrusted with the salt that makes those waters utterly unfit to drink. And as the traveler wanders around the spot, he is irresistibly reminded of the time when "the LORD rained upon Sodom and upon Gomorrah brimstone and fire from the LORD out of heaven; And he overthrew those cities, and all the plain, and all the inhabitants of the cities, and that which grew upon the ground" (Gen. 19:24–25).

REASONS THAT JUSTIFIED
THIS DIVINE JUDGMENT

(1) *It was a merciful warning to the rest of mankind.* The lesson of Noah's flood had nearly faded from the memory of man, and heedless of all restraint, the human family had made terrible advances in the course of open, shameless vice. It was so bad that there seemed an imminent danger of men repeating the abominable crimes that had opened the channels of the deluge. It was surely, therefore, wise and merciful to set up a warning that told its own dreadful story and reminded transgressors that there were limits beyond which the Judge of all the earth would not permit them to go.

It is true that the visitation, if it temporarily alarmed the nations of the immediate neighborhood, did not prevent them from reaching a similar excess of immorality some centuries later or from incurring at the edge of Joshua's sword the doom that heaven's fire had executed on their neighbors in the Jordan plain. Still, God's warnings have a merciful intention, even where they are unheeded, and this Sodom catastrophe has been well said to belong to that class of terrors in which a wise man will trace God's loving-kindness. "Whoso is wise, and will observe these things, even they will understand the lovingkindness of the LORD" (Ps. 107:43).

(2) *Moreover, in this terrible act the Almighty simply hastened the result of their own actions.* As the northeast wind that snaps the forest trees only hastens the result for which the borer-worm had already prepared, nations are not destroyed until they are rotten at the core. It would have been clear to any thoughtful observer who had ventured out after dark in Sodom that it must inevitably fall. Unnatural crime had already eaten out the national heart, and in the ordinary course of events, utter collapse could not be long delayed.

Go into the tents of Abraham, and you find simplicity, hospitality, and the graces of a truly noble character that guarantee the perpetuity of his name and the glorious future of his children. Then travel on to Sodom. In that sultry climate you find a population debilitated with luxury, debased by cowardly submission to a foreign tyrant, wounded to the core with vice, having not ten righteous men among them all, while the purity and sanctity of home are frivolous words. All these symptoms prognosticate, with prophetic voice, that their "judgment now of a long time lingereth not, and their damnation slumbereth not" (2 Pet. 2:3).

This suggests a solemn lesson for us. The tide of empires has ever moved westward. India, Babylon, Egypt, Greece, and Rome have successively wielded supreme power and sunk into oblivion. Shall it depart from Britain, as it has departed from the rest? It need not do so. Yet the ominous signs are all there: the increase of extravagance and luxury, the reckless expenditure on pleasure, the shameless vice that flaunts itself in our streets, the adulation of wealth, the devotion to gambling, the growing laxness of the marriage vows. I may well entertain the darkest fears about the future of my fatherland. The only hope for us is based on the important part that we are called to play in facilitating the evangelization of the world. Should we fail in this, nothing can avert our fall.

(3) *Besides, this overthrow happened only after careful investigation.* "I will go down now, and see" (Gen. 18:21). Beneath these simple words we catch a glimpse of one of the most sacred principles of divine action. God does not act hastily nor upon hearsay evidence. He must see for Himself if there may not be some mitigating or extenuating circumstances. It was only after He had come to the fig tree for many years, seeking fruit in vain, that He said, "Cut it down; why cumbereth it the ground?" (Luke 13:7). And this deliberation is a characteristic of God, who is unwilling that any should perish, who is slow to anger. Judgment is His inexplicable work. He tells us that someday, when we come to look into His doings, we shall be comforted concerning many of the evils that He has brought on the world, because we shall know that He has not done *without cause* all that He has done (Eze. 14:23).

(4) *There is this consideration also, that during the delay, many a warning was sent.* First, there was the conquest by Chedorlaomer, some twenty years before the time of which we write. Then there

was the presence of Lot, which, indeed, was weakened by his inconsistencies but was yet a protest on the behalf of righteousness (2 Pet. 2:7–8). Finally, there was the deliverance and restoration by the forceful intervention of Abraham. Again and again God had warned the men of these cities of their inevitable doom if they did not repent. To use His own expressive words, He "rose up early" to send His messengers, but the people would not hear.

Nor is His usage different in the case of individuals. The course of every sin is against a succession of menacing red lights and blaring fog signals warning of danger if that course is pursued. Just as the quivering of the nerves tells when the system is overstrained and demands immediate rest at the risk of certain paralysis, if that warning is disregarded, so God has arranged that no downward step in sin can be taken without setting off vast numbers of shrill bells that tell of danger ahead. Transgressor, the signals are all against you!

To heed these alarms is to be saved. To disregard them, persevering in spite of all, is to deaden the soul, harden the heart, and run the risk of blasphemy against the Holy Ghost. Keep in mind that the unpardonable sin is not an act but a state—the condition of the soul that does not and cannot feel, that is utterly insensible and careless of its state, that drifts heedless to its doom and is not forgiven simply because it does not admit or feel its need of forgiveness and therefore does not ask for it.

(5) *It is worthy of notice that God saved all whom He could.* Lot was a sorry wreck of a noble beginning. When he began as Abraham's companion from Ur, Lot gave promise of a life of quite unusual power and fruit. But he was one of those characters who cannot stand success. There is no temptation more insidious or perilous than success. The Enchanted Ground is more to be dreaded than the open assaults of Apollyon. More are ruined by the deceitfulness of riches than by the cares of life.

When Lot first went down to Sodom, attracted by the sole consideration of its pastures, it was no doubt his intention to keep aloof from its people and to live outside its walls. But the moth cannot flutter about the flame without being burned. By and by, Lot abandoned the tent and took a house inside the city. At last he betrothed his daughters to native Sodomites and sat in its gateway as one of its aldermen. He was given to hospitality, but in the proposals by which he endeavored to uphold its exercise, he proved how the air of Sodom had taken the bloom of his purity (Gen. 19:8). He was with difficulty dragged out of Sodom, as a brand plucked from the burning, and over the closing scenes of his life it is fitting to draw a veil. And yet such a wreck was saved!

Nor was he saved alone. But his wife did not take many steps outside the city before she showed herself utterly hopeless by looking back with a mixture of disobedience and regret. And Lot's two daughters made it out of Sodom only to behave so indecently that their names are branded with eternal infamy. If God was so careful to secure their safety, how bad must those have been whom He left to their fate! Is it not clear that He saved all who came within the range of mercy's possibilities? There will not be one soul among the lost who had the faintest claim to be among the saved, and there will be a great many among the saved whose presence there will be a very great surprise to us. "That many shall come from the east and west,...But the children of the kingdom shall be cast out into outer darkness" (Matt. 8:11–12).

THE MOTIVES OF THE ANGELS' VISIT

These were three:

(1) *The immediate cause was their own love to man.* The angels love us. Though they know that we are destined to a dignity before which that of the loftiest seraphs must pale, no envy eats out the pure benevolence that throbs within their holy spirits. It is enough that God has willed it so and that we are dear to their sweet Master, Christ. It is then no hardship for them to leave their golden palaces to come and hasten lingerers to repentance. If there is any hardship, it is when their mission is to destroy.

(2) *The efficient cause was Abraham's prayer.* "And it came to pass, when God destroyed the cities of the plain, that God remembered Abraham, and sent Lot out of the midst of the overthrow" (Gen. 19:29). Pray on, beloved reader, pray on for that dear one far away in the midst of a very Sodom of iniquity. It may seem impossible for you to go down into it for his rescue or to help him in any other way. But in answer to your prayer, God will send His angels to that ship laboring in mid-ocean, into that log house in the Canadian clearing or that shanty by an African diamond mine, or away to that place dedicated to vice and drink. God's angels go everywhere. A Sodom cannot hold its victims back from an angel's

touch, anymore than an angel's bright presence can be soiled by the polluting atmosphere through which it passes. While you are praying, God's angels are on their way to perform your desire, albeit that their progress may be hindered by causes hidden from our understanding (Dan. 10:12).

(3) *But the ultimate cause was God's mercy.* "The LORD being merciful unto him" (Gen. 19:16). Mercy is the last link in the chain. There is nothing beyond it. The apostle Paul cannot allege a more comprehensive or satisfactory reason for his position in the sunlit circle of salvation than this: "I obtained mercy" (1 Tim. 1:16). "By the grace of God I am what I am" (1 Cor. 15:10). And this shall be our theme also through that eternity whose daystar has already arisen in our hearts.

It seems marvelous that God should employ sons of men to win men to Himself. Surely angels could do it better! Nay, did they not save Lot with a perseverance and a holy ingenuity that is full of instruction for us as workers for the Lord? The world is full of Sodoms still. And Lots, whom we have known and loved or who have a claim on us, are sitting at their gates. Why are we behind the angels in eagerness to pluck them as brands from the burning? Bright spirits, you shall read us some holy lessons as to methods of Christian work, and we will try to emulate you.

THE ANGELS WENT TO WHERE LOT WAS

"And there came two angels to Sodom at even" (Gen. 19:1). What! Did angels go to Sodom? Yes, to Sodom—and yet angels. And as a ray of light may pass through the fetid atmosphere of some filthy court and emerge without a stain on its pure texture, so may angels spend a night in Sodom, surrounded by crowds of sinners and yet be untainted angels still. If you go to Sodom for your gains, as Lot did, you will soon show signs of moral pollution. But if you go to save men, as these angels did, you may go into a very hell of evil, where the air is laden with impurity and blasphemy, but you will not be defiled. No grain of mud shall stick. "No weapon that is formed against thee shall prosper; and every tongue that shall rise against thee in judgment thou shalt condemn" (Isa. 54:17).

This is the spirit of Christ's gospel. "Go after that which is lost, until he find it" (Luke 15:4). "Jesus put forth his hand, and touched him" (Matt. 8:3). We must not wait for sinners to come to us; we must go to them—to the banks of the stream where the fish hide in the dark, cool depths; to the highways of the town where men congregate; to restaurants, orchestra halls, dark taverns, and homes of poverty; yes, and to the most distant parts of the world. Wherever men are found, we must go to them and preach the gospel. The most unlikely places will yield Lots, who would have died in their sins if they had not been sought out.

They Were Content to Work for Very Few

Special value is attached to handpicked fruit. Too often we, in our ignorance, prefer to go into the orchard and shake down from the trees the abundant crop until the ground far and near is littered with fruit. But we forget how much waste there is in the process and how much of the crop becomes bruised, while some of it is torn prematurely from the parent branch.

So far as we can gather, all our Lord's finest followers were the result of His personal ministry. To one and another He said, "Follow Me!" His life was full of personal interviews where He sought out individual souls (Matt. 4:19, 21; 9:9; Luke 19:5). He would spend much time and thought to win one solitary woman whose character was none too good (John 4). He believed in going after one sheep that was lost. And the steadfastness of their characters vindicated His methods. It is most beautiful to trace the same characteristic in the apostle Paul, who says that he was "warning every man, and teaching every man in all wisdom; that we may present every man perfect in Christ Jesus" (Col. 1:28).

It is a question whether more men are saved by individual appeal than by all our preaching. It is not the sermon that wins them but the quiet talk with a worker after a service, or the letter of a parent, or the words of a friend. When Christ said, "Preach the gospel to every creature," did He not suggest that we were to set ourselves to the work of leaving the proclamation of heaven's love at every door and to every child of Adam throughout the world?

We never know what we accomplish when we win one soul for God. Is not the following story, drawn from the biography of James Brainerd Taylor—called home to God too early and yet not before he had won hundreds of souls by his personal appeals—a fair example of myriads more?

On one occasion, Taylor reined up his horse to drink at a roadside well. Another horseman at the same moment did the same. The servant of God, as the horses were eagerly quenching their thirst, turned to the stranger and spoke some burning words concerning the duty and honor of Christian discipleship. After a few minutes, they had parted and were riding in different directions, but the word of God remained as incorruptible seed and led to the conversion of that wayside hearer, who became a Christian and a missionary. Often he wondered who had been the instrument of his conversion and sought for him in vain. But he did not succeed in identifying him till years after, when, in a packet of books sent to him from his native land, he opened the story of that devoted life and in the front of the book beheld the face that had haunted him in sleeping and waking hours ever since that short but memorable interview.

It has been said that the best method of soul winning is to set your heart on some one soul and to pursue it until it has either definitely accepted or finally rejected the gospel of the grace of God. We should not hear so many cries for larger circles if Christians only realized the possibilities of the humblest life. Christ found work enough in a village to keep Him there for thirty years. Philip was torn from the great revival in Samaria to go into the desert to win one seeker after God.

Have you ever spoken to your employee, your child's teacher, your postman, your companion, your neighbor? It would not take long to evangelize the world if every man would teach his neighbor and every man his brother, saying, "Know the Lord!"

They Told Lot plainly of His Danger

"Hast thou here any besides?... bring them out of this place: For we will destroy this place, because the cry of them is waxen great before the face of the LORD; and the LORD hath sent us to destroy it" (Gen. 19:12–13). We are rather timid nowadays of talking to men this way. We have lined our lips with velvet. We aim to be gentler than Christ. He did not hesitate to speak of an undying worm and a quenchless flame. The gnashing of teeth, the wail of despair, and the knock to which no door would open were arguments that came more than once from His lips. (See Matt. 8:12; 13:42, 50; 22:13; 24:51; 25:10–12, 30; Mark 9:43–48; Luke 8:25–28.) He evidently taught as if men might make a mistake that they could not possibly repair. If certain basics are lacking in food, children will grow up unhealthy; and if we do not take care, the deficiency of our modern teaching will have disastrous results. Whether we talk about it or not, it is still as true as the nature of God that those who obey not the gospel of our Lord Jesus Christ "shall be punished with everlasting destruction from the presence of the Lord, and from the glory of his power" (2 Thess. 1:9). And "if we sin wilfully after that we have received the knowledge of the truth, there remaineth no more sacrifice for sins, but a certain fearful looking for of judgment and fiery indignation, which shall devour the adversaries" (Heb. 10:26–27).

It may be that the final day of grace is nearer to its close than we think. The clock of destiny may have struck. The avalanche may have commenced to roll forward its overwhelming mass, while the storm clouds may brood heavily over a godless age, for which, in the day of judgment, it shall be worse than for Sodom and Gomorrah. There may be nothing to foretell this momentous fact. "The sun was risen upon the earth when Lot entered into Zoar" (Gen. 19:23). Nature keeps God's secrets well. No sign in heaven, no billowing thunderhead in the clouds, no tremor on earth, but the ax suddenly driven home to the heart of the doomed tree. Escape, my reader, for your life; look not behind you, neither stay anywhere short of the cleft side of Jesus, where only we may hide from the just judgment of sin. Rest not till you have put the Lord Jesus between yourself and the footsteps of pursuing justice.

They Hastened Him

"And when the morning arose, then the angels hastened Lot" (Gen. 19:15). The angels had been reluctant to stay in his house, unlike the swiftness with which they accepted Abraham's hospitality. And they spent the short, sultry night in persuading Lot about the certainty and terror of the approaching destruction. So much so that they actually got him to go to arouse his sons-in-law. But a compromising life cannot arrest the wanderer or startle the sleeper into wide-awakeness about his soul. People say that we must conform a little to the manners of our time if we would exert a saving influence over men. It is a fatal mistake. If we live in Sodom, we shall have no power to save the people of Sodom. You must stand outside of them if you would save them from the gurgling rapids.

Yes, dwellers in Sodom, you cannot level Sodom up, but it will certainly level you down and laugh at you when you try to speak. "But he seemed as one that mocked unto his sons in law" (Gen. 19:14).

But when he came back from his ineffectual mission, Lot seemed infected by the skepticism that had ridiculed his warnings. "He lingered" (Gen. 19:16). How could he leave his children and household goods and property on what seemed to be a fool's errand? Surely all things would continue as they had been from the beginning of the world. "And while he lingered, the men laid hold upon his hand."

It was hand help. It was the urgency of a love that would take no denial. The two angels had but four hands, but each hand was full, and each clasped the hand of a procrastinating sinner. Would that we knew more fully this divine enthusiasm that pulls men out of the fire (Jude 23)!

Nor were they satisfied until their *proteges* were safe outside the city and were speeding toward the bulwark of the distant hills. So Lot was saved from the overthrow. But though he was sent out of Sodom, he took Sodom with him, and over the remainder of his history we must draw a veil. Still, it is a marvelous testimony to the power of intercessory prayer to learn that a man so low in the moral scale, together with his daughters, was saved for Abraham's sake. And if Lot had finally settled at the little city of Zoar, that, too, would have been spared for his sake.

Let us hasten sinners. Let us say to each one: "Escape for your life. Better to lose all you value than to lose your soul. Look not behind to past attainments or failures. Linger nowhere outside the City of Refuge, which is Jesus Christ Himself. Hasten on! Habits of indecision strengthen; opportunities are closing in; the arrow of destruction has already left the bow of justice." "Behold, now is the accepted time; behold, now is the day of salvation" (2 Cor. 6:2).

18

A BIT OF
THE OLD NATURE

Then Abimelech called Abraham, and said unto him,
What hast thou done unto us? and what have I offended thee,
that thou hast brought on me and on my kingdom a great sin?
Genesis 20:9

*F*or long years, an evil may lurk in our hearts, permitted and unjudged, breeding failure and sorrow in our lives, as some unnoticed and forgotten sewer may secretly undermine the health of an entire household. In the twilight we overlook many things that we would not allow for a single moment if we saw it in its true character. Under the all-revealing light of the perfect day, we would be the first to fling it away in horror. But that which escapes our sight is conspicuous in all its naked deformity to the eye of God. "The darkness and the light are both alike to thee" (Ps. 139:12). And He will so direct the discipline of our lives as to set in clear prominence the deadly evil that He hates, so that when He has laid bare the cancerous growth, He may bring us to long for and invite the knife that shall set us free from it forever.

These words have been suggested by the thirteenth verse of this twentieth chapter, which indicates an evil agreement into which Abraham had entered with Sarah some thirty years before the time of which we write. Addressing the king of the Philistines, the patriarch let fall a hint that sheds a startling light upon his failure when he first entered the land of promise and, under stress of famine, went down into Egypt. It is the repetition of his failure that we must now consider. Here is what he said: "And it came to pass, when God caused me to wander from my father's house, that I said unto her, This is thy kindness which thou shalt show unto me; at every place whither we shall come, say of me, He is my brother."

In a certain sense, no doubt, Sarah was his sister. She was the daughter of his father, though not the daughter of his mother. But she was much more his wife than his sister, and to withhold that fact was to withhold the one fact that was essential to the maintenance of his honor and the protection of her virtue. We are not bound to tell the whole truth to gratify an idle curiosity, but we are bound not to withhold the one item that another should know before completing a bargain if the knowledge of it would materially alter the result. A lie consists in the motive quite as much as in the actual words. We may unwittingly say that which is actually false, meaning above all things to speak the truth, and, though a lie in kind, there is no lie in fact. On the other hand, like Abraham, we may utter true words, meaning them to convey a false impression, and in the sight of heaven, we are guilty of a deliberate and shameful falsehood.

This secret compact between Abraham and his wife, in the earliest days of his exodus, was due to his slender faith in God's power to take care of them, which again sprang from his limited experience of his Almighty Friend. In this we may find its sole excuse. But long before this, it should have been canceled by mutual consent. The faithless treaty should have been torn into shreds and scattered to the winds of heaven. It was not enough that they did not act on it for many years, for it was evidently still in existence, tacitly admitted by each of them, and only waiting for an emergency to arise from the dusty obscurity into which it had receded and to come again into light and use.

But the existence of this hidden understanding, though perhaps Abraham did not realize it, was inconsistent with the relation into which he had now entered with God. It was altogether a source of weakness and failure. And above all, it was the secret flaw in his faith that would inevitably affect its tone and destroy its effectiveness in the dark trials that were approaching. God could afford to pass it over in those early days when faith itself was yet in inception, but it could not be permitted when that faith was reaching to a maturity in which any flaw would be instantly detected. It would be an unsuitable example in one who was to become the model of faith to the world.

The judgment and eradication of this lurking evil were therefore necessary, and they were brought about in this way.

The day before Sodom's fall, the Almighty told Abraham that at a set time in the following year, he should have a son and heir. And we would have expected that he would have spent the slow-moving months beneath the oak of Mamre, already hallowed by so many associations. But such was not the case. It has been suggested that he was too horrified at the overthrow of the cities of the plain to be able to remain any longer in the vicinity. All further association with the spot was distasteful to him. Or it may have been that another famine was threatening. But in any case, "Abraham journeyed from thence towards the south country, and dwelled between Kadesh and Shur, and sojourned in Gerar" (Gen. 20:1).

Gerar was the capital of a race of men who had dispossessed the original inhabitants of the land. They were gradually passing from the condition of a wandering shepherd life into that of a settled and warlike nation. Later they became known to the Hebrews by the dreaded name, Philistines, a title which, in fact, gave to the whole land its name of Palestine. Their chieftain bore the official title of Abimelech, "My Father the King."

Here, the almost forgotten agreement between Sarah and Abraham offered itself as a ready contrivance behind which Abraham's unbelief took shelter. Abraham knew the ungoverned license of his time, unbridled by the fear of God (vs. 11). He dreaded, lest the heathen monarch, enamored with Sarah's beauty or ambitious to get her into his power for purposes of state policy, might slay him for his wife's sake. And so he again resorted to the flimsy policy of calling her his sister. He acted as if God could not have defended him and her, screening them from evil as He had done so often in days gone by.

His Conduct was Very Cowardly

He risked Sarah's virtue and the purity of the promised seed. And even if we accept the justification of his conduct proposed by some, who argue that he was so sure of the seed promised him by God that he could dare to risk what otherwise he would have more carefully guarded, and thus his faith led him into the license of presumption, it was surely very mean on his part to permit Sarah to pass through any ordeal of the sort. If he had such superabundant faith, he might have risked his own safety at the hand of Abimelech rather than Sarah's virtue.

It Was also very Dishonoring to God

Among those heathen tribes, Abraham was well known as the servant of Jehovah. They could only judge the character of Him whom they could not see by the traits they discerned in His servant, whom they knew in a customary fashion. Alas, that Abraham's standard was lower than their own, so much so that Abimelech was able to rebuke him, saying: "Thou hast brought on me and on my kingdom a great sin? thou hast done deeds unto me that ought not to be done" (Gen. 20:9). Such an opinion, elicited in such a way, must have been an inauspicious preparation for any attempt to proselytize Abimelech to the Hebrew faith. "Not so," we can imagine him saying. "I have had some experience of one of its foremost representatives, and I prefer to remain as I am."

It is heartbreaking when the heathen rebukes a professor of superior godliness for speaking lies. Yet it is lamentable to confess that such men often have higher standards of morality than those who profess godliness. Even if they do not fulfill their own conceptions, yet the beauty of their ideal is undeniable and is a remarkable vindication of the universal vitality of conscience. The self-controlled Hindu is scandalized by the drunkenness of the Englishman whose religion he is invited to embrace. The Chinese cannot understand why they should exchange the ancient religion of Confucius for that of a people that by superior military power forces upon their country a drug that is sapping its life away. The employee abhors a creed that is professed by his boss for one day of the week but is disowned on the other six. Let us walk carefully toward those who are not believers, adorning in all things the gospel of Jesus Christ and giving no occasion to the enemy to blaspheme.

IT ALSO STOOD IN CONTRAST
TO THE BEHAVIOR OF ABIMELECH

As to his original character, Abimelech commends himself to us as the nobler of the two. He rises early in the morning, prompt to set the great wrong right. He warns his people. He restores Sarah with bountiful presents. His reproach and rebuke are spoken in the gentlest, kindest tones. He simply tells Sarah that her position as the wife of a prophet would, not in Philistia only but wherever they might come, be a sufficient security and veil (Gen. 20:16). There is the air of high-minded nobility in his behavior throughout this crisis that is exceedingly charming.

It would almost appear as if the Spirit of God took delight in showing that the original texture of God's saints was not higher than that of other men, nor indeed so high. What they became, they became in spite of their natural selves. So marvelous is the wonder-working power of the grace of God that He can graft His rarest fruits on the wildest stocks. He seems to delight to secure His choicest results in natures that men of the world might reject as hopelessly bad. He demands no assistance from us, so sure is He that when faith is admitted as the root principle of character, all other things will be added to it.

Oh, critics of God's handiwork, we do not deny the inconsistencies of a David, a Peter, or an Abraham. However, we insist that those inconsistencies were not the result of God's work but in spite of it. They indicate the hopelessness of the original nature—the moorland waste to which He has set His cultivating hand. And shall we blame the Gardener's skill when, in the paradise that He has created, we encounter a bit of original soil, which, by force of contrast, indicates the marvel of His genius? If we exercise patience as we observe His skill, He will work the same spell upon us, and we will blossom as the rest.

And you, on the other hand, who aspire for the crown of saintliness to which you are truly called, take heart! There is nothing that God has done for any soul that He will not do for you. There is no soil so unpromising that He will not compel it to yield His fairest results. "The things which are impossible with men are possible with God" (Luke 18:27). The same power in all its matchless energy that raised the body of our Lord from its sleep in the grave of Joseph to sit at the Father's side in the heights of glory, in spite of opposing battalions of evil spirits, is ready to do as much for each of us if only we will daily, hourly, yield to it without reserve. Only cease from your own works and keep always on God's "lift," refusing every appeal to step off its ascending energy or to do for yourself what He will do for you so much better than you can ask or think.

Let us ponder, as we close, these practical lessons:

(1) *We are never safe as long as we are in this world.* Abraham was an old man. Thirty years had passed since that sin had shown itself last. During that time, he had been growing and learning much. But, alas, the snake was hindered but not killed! The weeds were cut down, not eradicated! The dry rot had been checked, but the rotten timbers had not been cut away! Once-cherished sins are kept in check only by God's grace. If you cease to abide in Christ, they will revive and revisit you as the seven sleepers of Ephesus reappeared to the panic-stricken town.

(2) *We have no right to throw ourselves into the way of the temptation that has often mastered us.* Those who daily cry "Lead us not into temptation" should see to it that they do not court the temptation against which they pray. We must not expect angels to catch us every time we choose to cast ourselves from the mountain brow. A godly fear will avoid the perilous pass marked by crosses to indicate the failures of the past and will choose a safer route. Abraham had been wiser had he never gone into the Philistines' territory at all.

(3) *We may be encouraged by God's treatment of Abraham's sin.* Although God had a secret controversy with His child, He did not put him away. And when his wife and he were in extreme danger, as the result of his sin, their Almighty Friend stepped in to deliver them from the peril that menaced them. Again "he reproved kings for their sakes, saying, Touch not mine anointed, and do my prophets no harm" (1 Chron. 16:21–22). Indeed, He told Abimelech that he was a dead man and put an apprehension upon him by the means of an ominous disease, telling him to ask for the intercession of the very man by whom he had been so grievously misled and who, in spite of all his failures, was a prophet still, having power with God.

Have you sinned, bringing disrepute on the name of God? Do not despair. Go alone, as Abraham must have done, and confess your sin with tears and childlike trust. Do not abandon prayer. Your prayers are still sweet to Him. He waits to answer them. It is only through them that His purposes can be fulfilled toward men. Trust then in the patience and forgiveness of God, and let His love, as consuming fire, rid you of concealed and hidden sin.

19

HAGAR AND
ISHMAEL CAST OUT

Cast out this bondwoman and her son:
for the son of this bondwoman
shall not be heir...with Isaac.
Genesis 21:10

*E*ven though we were hearing this story for the first time and did not know of the grave crisis to which we were approaching in Genesis 22, we might be sure that something of the sort was imminent. We should rest our conclusion on the fact of the stern discipline through which the great patriarch was called to pass. Faith is the expression of our inner moral life, and it cannot be exercised in its loftiest form as long as there is any crookedness of the heart, any hidden or unholy affection. These things must be cut away or passed through the fiery discipline of sorrow, that, being freed from them, the heart may exercise that supreme faith in God that is the fairest crown of human existence.

The Almighty Lover of souls knew the trial that awaited His child in the near future and set Himself to prepare Abraham for it by ridding him of certain clinging inconsistencies that would have paralyzed the action of his faith in the hour of trial. We have already seen how one of these—the secret agreement between himself and Sarah—was exposed to the light and judged. We have now to see how another matter, the patriarch's connection with Hagar and her child, was also dealt with by Him, who acts on us either as fullers' soap or, if that is not strong enough, as a refiner's fire (Mal. 3:2).

In what way the presence of Hagar and Ishmael hindered the development of Abraham's noblest life of faith we cannot entirely understand. Did Abraham's heart still cling to the girl who had given him his firstborn son? Was there any secret satisfaction in the arrangement that had at least achieved one cherished purpose, though it had been unblessed by God? Was there any fear that if he was summoned to surrender Isaac, he would find it easier to do so because, at any moment, he could fall back on Ishmael as both son and heir? We cannot read all that was in Abraham's mind, but surely some such thoughts are suggested by the expressions that this hour records as the history of the anguish of this torn and lonely heart. One darling idol after another was rent away, that Abraham might be cast naked and helpless on the omnipotence of the Eternal God. "And the thing was very grievous in Abraham's sight" (Gen. 21:11).

It may be that you desire to possess a faith like Abraham's—a faith that staggers not through unbelief, a faith to which God cannot give a denial, a faith that can open and shut heaven, and to which all things are possible. But are you willing to pay the cost— the cost of suffering, the cost of rending from your heart all that would frustrate the operation of so glorious a principle, the cost of seeing one cherished idol after another cast out, the cost of being stripped even to nakedness of all the dear delights in which the flesh may have found pleasure? "Are ye able to drink of the cup that I shall drink of, and to be baptized with the baptism that I am baptized with? They say unto him, We are able" (Matt. 20:22). You hardly realize all that is meant when you say so much, but it shall be revealed to you step by step. And nothing shall be too difficult, all being measured out according to your strength by Him who knows our frame and remembers that we are dust. Let us not dread the pruning knife, for it is wielded by the hand of One who loves us infinitely and who is seeking results that are to fill our hearts with eternal gratitude and heaven with praise.

The final separation from Abraham of elements that would have been injurious to the exercise of a supreme faith was brought about by the birth of the long promised child, which is alluded to at the commencement of this chapter (Gen. 21) and which led up to the crisis with which we are now dealing.

"And the LORD visited Sarah as he had said, and the LORD did unto Sarah as he had spoken" (Gen. 21:1). It is impossible to trust God too absolutely. God's least word is a beam of imperishable wood driven into the Rock of Ages, which will never give and on which you may hang your entire weight forevermore. "The counsel of the LORD standeth for ever, the thoughts of his heart to all generations" (Ps. 33:11).

BUT WE MUST BE
PREPARED TO WAIT GOD'S TIME

"Sarah conceived, and bare Abraham a son in his old age, at the set time of which God had spoken unto him" (Gen. 21:2). God has His set times. It is not for us to know them; indeed, we cannot know them; we must wait for them. If God had told Abraham in Haran that he must wait for thirty years until he pressed the promised child to his bosom, his heart would have failed him. So, in gracious love, the length of the weary years was hidden, and only as they were nearly spent and there were only a few more months to wait, God told him that "according to the time of life, and Sarah shall have a son" (Gen. 18:14). The set time came at last, and then the laughter that filled the patriarch's home made the aged pair forget the long and weary vigil. "And Abraham called the name of his son that was born unto him, whom Sarah bare to him, Isaac" (that is *Laughter*, Gen. 21:3). Take heart, waiting one, you wait for One who cannot disappoint you. He will not be five minutes behind the appointed moment when "your sorrow shall be turned into joy" (John 16:20).

"A woman when she is in travail hath sorrow, because her hour is come: but as soon as she is delivered of the child, she remembereth no more the anguish, for joy that a man is born into the world" (John 16:21). That joy may give the clue to the unusual outburst of song on the part of the happy and aged mother. The laughter of disbelief with which she received the first suggestion of her approaching motherhood (Gen. 18:12) was now exchanged for the laughter of fulfilled hope. And she gave utterance to words that approached the elevation of a rhythmic chant, serving as the model of that other song with which the virgin mother announced the advent of her Lord. So Sarah said, "*God hath made me to laugh, so that all that hear will laugh with me*" (Gen. 21:6).

And long after, one of her daughters said, "*My soul doth magnify the Lord, and my spirit hath rejoiced in God my Saviour.... For he that is mighty hath done to me great things; and holy is his name*" (Luke 1:46–49).

Ah, happy soul, when God makes you laugh! Then sorrow and crying shall flee away forever, as darkness before the dawn.

The peace of Abraham's house remained at first unbroken, though there may have been some slight symptoms of the rupture that was at hand. The dislike that Sarah had manifested to Hagar long years before had never been extinguished. It had only lodged in her bosom, waiting for some slight incident to stir it again into a blaze. Nor had the warm passionate nature of Hagar ever forgotten those hard dealings that had driven her forth to fare as best she might in the inhospitable desert. Abraham must have been often sorely put to it to keep the peace between them. At last the women's quarters could conceal the quarrel no longer, and the scandal broke out into the open day.

THE IMMEDIATE OCCASION OF THIS BREACH

"The child grew, and was weaned: and Abraham made a great feast the same day that Isaac was weaned" (Gen. 21:8). But amid all the bright joy of that happy occasion, one shadow suddenly stole over the scene and brooded on the mother's soul. Sarah's vigilant eye saw Ishmael mocking. It was hardly to be wondered at. The lad had recently suffered a severe disappointment. He had grown up as the undisputed heir of all that camp, accustomed to receive its undivided loyalty, and it must have been very difficult to view with equanimity the preparations made in honor of the child who was destined to supersede him. So, under the appearance of sportive jesting, he jeered at Isaac in a way that betrayed the bitterness of his soul that he had been careful to conceal. This awoke all of Sarah's slumbering jealousy that may have often been severely tested during the past few years by Ishmael's arrogance and independent bearing. She would stand it no longer. Why should she, the chieftain's wife and mother of his heir, submit to the insolence of a slave?

And so she said unto Abraham with the sting of the old jealousy, "Cast out this bondwoman and her son: for the son of this bondwoman shall not be heir with my son, even with Isaac" (Gen. 21:10).

HOW THE GREAT APOSTLE UNDERSTOOD THIS INCIDENT

In Paul's time, the Jews, priding themselves on being the descendants of Abraham, refused to consider it possible that any but themselves could be children of God and the heirs of promise. They appropriated to themselves exclusive privileges and position. When large numbers of Gentiles were born into the Christian Church under the first preaching of the gospel and were proclaimed to be the spiritual seed, they who, like Ishmael, were simply "born after the flesh persecuted him that was born after the Spirit," like Isaac. Everywhere the Jews set themselves to resist the preaching of the gospel, attempting to deny new converts of their exclusive privileges and to harass those who would not enter the Church through the rites of Judaism. Before long, the Jewish nation was rejected, put aside, and cast out. Succeeding ages have seen the growth of the Church from among the once-persecuted ones, while the children of Abraham have wandered in the wilderness fainting for the true water of life (Gal. 4:29).

BUT THERE IS A STILL DEEPER REFERENCE

Hagar, the slave, who may even have been born in the Sinaitic Desert with which she seems to have been so familiar, is a fitting representative of the spirit of legalism and bondage that seeks to win spiritual life by the observance of the law, which was given from those same old cliffs. Hagar is the covenant made on Mount Sinai in Arabia "which gendereth to bondage,...and is in bondage with her children" (Gal. 4:24–25). Sarah, the free woman, on the other hand, represents the covenant of free grace. Her children are love and faith and hope; they are bound not by the spirit of "must" but by the promptings of spontaneous gratitude; their home is not in the frowning clefts of Sinai, but in Jerusalem above, which *is* free and is the mother of us all (Gal. 4:26). Now, argues the apostle, there was no room for Hagar and Sarah, with their respective children, in Abraham's tent. If Ishmael was there, it was because Isaac was not born. But as soon as Isaac came in, Ishmael must go out.

149

So the two principles—of the legalism that insists on the performance of the outward rite of circumcision and of the faith that accepts the finished work of the Savior—cannot coexist in one heart. It is a moral impossibility. As well could darkness coexist with light, and slavery with freedom. So, addressing the Galatian converts, who were being tempted by Judaizing teachers to mingle legalism and faith, the apostle Paul directed them to follow the example of Abraham by casting out the spirit of bondage that keeps the soul in one perpetual agony of unrest (Gal. 4:30).

I trust that you are trusting Christ, but perhaps you are living in perpetual bondage to a code of religious performance that you feel pleases God. Perhaps you are always endeavoring to add some acts of obedience as a way of completing and assuring your salvation. Ah, it is a great mistake! Cease to worry about these legal matters. Beware of morbid principles of conscience, one of the most terrible diseases by which the human spirit can be plagued. Do not ever imagine that God's love for you depends on the performance of many minute acts, concerning which there are no definite instructions given. Trust Christ. Realize His wonderful and complete salvation. Work not toward sonship but from it. "Cast out the bondwoman and her son." Live the free, happy life of Isaac, whose position is assured, and not that of Ishmael, whose position is dependent on his good behavior. "And the servant abideth not in the house for ever: but the Son abideth ever" (John 8:35).

The remaining history is briefly told. With many a heart pang—as the vine that bleeds copiously when the pruning knife is doing its work—Abraham sent Hagar and her child forth from his home, bidding them a last sad farewell. In the dim twilight, they went forth before the camp was astir. The strong man must have suffered keenly as he put the bread into her hand and with his own fingers bound the bottle of water on her shoulder, kissing Ishmael once more. And yet he must not let Sarah guess how much he felt it. How many passages in our lives are known only to God!

Yet it was better so. And God provided for them both. When Hagar's hopes were on the point of expiring and the lad lay dying of thirst in the scorching noon under the slender shade of a desert shrub, the angel of God interrupted her sobs, pointed out the well of water to which her tears had made her blind, and promised that her child should become a great nation. Ishmael would never have developed to his full stature if he had perpetually lived in the luxury of Abraham's camp. There was not room enough there for him to grow. For Ishmael, as for us all, there was need of the free air of the desert, where he should match himself with his peers, becoming strong by deprivation and need. What seems likely to break our hearts at this moment turns out in later years to have been of God. "And God said unto Abraham, Let it not be grievous in thy sight...in all that Sarah hath said unto thee, hearken unto her voice" (Gen. 21:12).

One more weight was laid aside from Abraham, and one more step taken in the preparation of God's "friend" for the supreme victory of his faith, for which his whole life had been a preparation and which was now at hand.

Some flowers are the result of a century of growth. The divine Gardener will consider Himself repaid for years of loving, patient care if the life He has tended will bloom out into but one act like that which we are soon to record. Such acts scatter the seeds of noble and heroic deeds for all future time.

20

A Quiet
Resting Place

And Abraham planted a grove in Beersheba,
and called there on the name of the LORD, the everlasting God.
And Abraham sojourned in the Philistines' land many days.
Genesis 21:33–34

*W*hen a river is approaching its plunge down
some mighty chasm, its waters flow with placid stillness; every
ripple is smoothed out of the peaceful surface, and the great volume
of water is hushed and quieted. There could hardly be a greater
contrast than that which exists between the restfulness of the river
before it is torn by the ragged rocks in its downward rush and its
excitement and foam at the foot of the falls. In the one case you can
discern through the clear waters the stones and rocks that line its
bed; in the other you are blinded by the spray and deafened by the
noise.

Is this not a symbol of our lives? Our Father often inserts in them
a parenthesis of rest and peace to prepare us for some coming trial.
It is not invariably so. We need not always temper our enjoyment

of some precious gift with a foreboding dread of what may follow it. But this, at least, is often true: if every season of sunshine is not followed by a time of clouds, yet seasons of sorrow and trial are almost always preceded by hours or days or years of sunny experience, which lie in the retrospect of life as a bright and comforting memory where the soul was able to gather the strength it was to expend and to prepare itself for its supreme effort.

Thus it happened to Abraham. We have already seen how wisely and tenderly his Almighty Friend had been preparing him for his approaching trial. First, there had been the exposure of his hidden compact with Sarah, and then the ridding him of the presence of Hagar and her son. And now some further preparation was to be wrought in his spirit through this period of peaceful rest beside the well of the oath. Leaving Gerar, the patriarch traveled with his slow-moving flocks along the fertile valley that extends from the sea into the country. The whole district was admirably suited for the maintenance of a vast pastoral clan. In the winter, the valley contains a running stream, and at any time, water may be obtained by digging at a greater or lesser depth. Having reached a suitable camping ground, Abraham dug a well, which is possibly one of those that remain to this day. The water, lying some forty feet below the surface, is pure and sweet. Drinking troughs for the use of cattle are scattered around in close proximity to the mouth, the curbstones of which are deeply worn by the friction of the ropes used in drawing up the water by hand. It is not improbable that these very stones were originally hewn under the patriarch's direction, even though their position may have been somewhat altered through the passage of time.

Shortly after Abraham had settled there, Abimelech, the king, accompanied by Phichol, the chief captain of his host, came to his encampment, intent on entering into a treaty that should be binding not only on themselves but also on their children: "Swear unto me here by God that thou wilt not deal falsely with me, nor with my son, nor with my son's son" (Gen. 21:23). Before formally binding himself under these solemn sanctions, Abraham brought up a matter that is still a fruitful subject of dispute in eastern lands. The herdsmen of Abimelech had violently taken away the well of water that the servants of Abraham had dug, but the king immediately repudiated all knowledge of their action. It had been done without his knowledge and sanction. And in the treaty into which the two chieftains entered, there was, so to speak, a special clause inserted with reference to this well, destined in later years to be so famous. Writing materials were not used, but the seven ewe lambs that Abraham gave Abimelech were the visible and lasting memorial that the well was his recognized property. Thus it happened that as the solemnly sworn covenant was made beside the well, so its name became forever associated with it and was called *Beersheba*, the well of the oath or "the well of the seven," with reference to the seven gifts on which the oath was taken.

In further commemoration of this treaty, Abraham planted a tamarisk tree, which, as a hardy evergreen, would long perpetuate the memory of the transaction in those lands where the mind of man eagerly searches for anything that will break the monotony of the landscape. There also he erected an altar and called on the name of the Lord, the Everlasting God. "And Abraham sojourned in the Philistines' land many days" (Gen. 21:34). Ah, those long, happy days! Their course was marked only by the growing years of Isaac, who passed on through the natural stages of growth—from boyhood to youth, and from youth to opening manhood—the object of Abraham's tender, clinging love. No words can tell the joy of Abraham over this beloved child of his old age. "Thine only son Isaac, whom thou lovest" (Gen. 22:2). It seemed as if perpetual laughter had come to take up its abode in that home, brightening the declining years of that aged pair. Who could have foretold that the greatest trial of all his life had yet to come and that from a clear sky a thunderbolt was about to fall, threatening to destroy all his happiness at a single stroke?

None of us know what awaits us. This at least is clear, that our life is being portioned out by the tender love of a God who spared not His own Son and has pledged Himself, with Him, also freely to give us all things (Rom. 8:32). Here is one of the unanswerable questions of Scripture: What will God not do for them that love Him? No love, no care, no wisdom, which they need, shall be spared. And yet, with all this, there may be acute suffering to bear. We sometimes forget that what God takes, He takes in fire. Nothing less than the discipline of pain can ever disintegrate the clinging dross of our nature. The only way to the resurrection life and the ascension mount is the way of the garden, the cross, and the grave.

Nothing will dare to inflict so much pain as the love that desires the richest and sweetest life for the object of its affection. "For whom the Lord loveth he chasteneth, and scourgeth every son whom he receiveth" (Heb. 12:6). Let us prepare, then, for coming hours of trial by doing as Abraham did.

LET US LIVE BY THE WELL

There is a great tendency among Christians today to magnify special places and scenes that have been associated with times of spiritual blessing and to obtain from them a supply that they store up for their maintenance in later days. But so many of these are in danger of forgetting that instead of making an annual pilgrimage to the well, they might take up their abode beside it and live there. The water of that well speaks of the life of God, which is in Jesus Christ our Lord and is stored up for us in the fathomless depths of the Word of God. The well is deep, yet faith's bucket can reach its precious contents and bring them to the thirsty lip and yearning heart.

One of the greatest blessings that can come to the soul is to acquire the habit of sinking wells into the depth that lies under and to draw water for itself. We are too much in the habit of drinking water that others have drawn and too little initiated into the sacred science of drawing for ourselves.

I think it would be more beneficial for Christians to not attempt to read so many chapters of the Bible daily but instead to study what they do read more carefully, turning to the marginal references, reading the context, comparing Scripture with Scripture, endeavoring to get one or more complete thoughts of the mind of God. I believe that a greater richness would come to their spiritual experience, more freshness in their interest in Scripture, more independence of men's teaching, and more real enjoyment of the Word of the living God. Oh, for a practical realization of what Jesus meant when He said: "The water that I shall give him shall be in him a well of water springing up into everlasting life" (John 4:14).

Oh, my readers, open your heart to the teaching of the Holy Ghost. Rest content with nothing short of a deep and loving knowledge of the Bible. Ask that within you there may be a repetition of the old miracle, "Then Israel sang this song, Spring up, O well; sing ye unto it" (Num. 21:17). Then "in the wilderness shall waters break out, and streams in the desert. And the parched ground shall become a pool, and the thirsty land springs of water" (Isa. 35:6–7).

LET US SHELTER BENEATH THE COVENANT

Abraham was quiet from the fear of evil because of Abimelech's oath. How much more sure and restful should be the believing soul that shelters beneath that everlasting covenant which is "ordered in all things, and sure" (2 Sam. 23:5). There are some Christians doubtful of their eternal salvation and fearful lest they should ultimately fall away from grace and be lost, to whom this advice is peculiarly appropriate: "Live by the well of the oath."

In the eternity of the past, the Eternal Father entered into covenant with His Son, the terms of which covenant seem to have been *in this manner*. On the one hand, our Lord pledged His complete obedience and His atoning death on behalf of all who would believe. And, on the other hand, the Father promised that all who believed in Him would be delivered from the penalty of a broken law, should be forgiven, adopted into His family, and saved with an eternal salvation. This is but a crude and inadequate statement of mysteries so fathomless that the loftiest seraphs peer into them in vain. And yet it sets forth, in the babbling of human language, a truth of the utmost importance, behind which the weakest believer may securely shelter.

The only question is, Do you believe in Jesus Christ? Or, to put it still more simply, Are you willing that the Holy Ghost should create in you a living faith in the Savior of men? *Would you believe if you could?* Is your will on God's side in this matter of faith? Are you prepared to surrender anything and everything that would hinder your simple-hearted faith in Jesus? If so, you may appropriate to yourself the blessings of the covenant confirmed by the counsel and oath of God. Your faith may be weak, but it is faith in its inception. And as Noah's ark saved the squirrel as well as the elephant, so does the covenant shelter the weakest and feeblest believer equally with the giant in faith.

This, then, becomes true of us if we believe. We are forgiven; our name is inscribed on the roll of the saved; we are adopted into the family of God; we have within us the beginning of a life that is eternal as the life of God. "For the mountains shall depart, and the hills be removed; but my kindness shall not depart from thee, neither shall the covenant of my peace be removed, saith the LORD that hath mercy on thee" (Isa. 54:10). And shall not this comfort us amid many a heartbreaking sorrow? Nothing can break the bonds by which our souls are knit with the eternal God. "Although my house be not so with God; yet he hath made with me an everlasting covenant, ordered in all things, and sure: for this is all my salvation, and all my desire, although he make it not to grow" (2 Sam. 23:5).

Rejoice in all the good things that the Lord your God gives you. Plant your trees; be comforted by their shade and fed by their fruit. Listen to the ringing laughter of your Isaac. Dread not the future, but trust the great love of God. Live by the well, and shelter beneath the covenant. So, if trial is approaching, you shall be the enabled to meet it with a calm and strong heart.

21

THE GREATEST TRIAL OF ALL

Take now thy son, thine only son Isaac,
whom thou lovest...and offer him there for a burnt offering.

Genesis 22:2

*A*s long as men live in the world, they will turn to this story with unwaning interest. The only scene in history by which it is surpassed is when the Great Father gave His Isaac to a death from which there was no deliverance. God and Abraham were friends in a common sorrow up to a certain point, though the infinite love of God stepped in to stay the hand of Abraham at the critical moment, sparing His friend what He would not spare Himself.

"GOD DID TEMPT ABRAHAM"

A better rendering might be, "God did put Abraham to the test." Satan tempts us that he may bring out the evil that is in our hearts, but God tries or tests us that He may bring out all the good. In the fiery trial through which the believer is called to pass, elements of evil that had counteracted his true development drop away, shriveled and consumed. Meanwhile, those latent qualities produced by grace but not yet brought into exercise are called to the front, receive due recognition, and acquire a fixity of position and influence that nothing else could possibly have given them. In the agony of sorrow, we say words and assume positions that otherwise we should never have dreamed of, but from which we never again recede. Looking back, we wonder how we dared to do as we did, and yet we are not sorry, because the memory of what we were in that supreme hour is a precious legacy as well as a platform from which we take a wider view and climb to the further heights that beckon us.

The common incidents of daily life, as well as the rare and exceptional crises, are so ordered as to give us incessant opportunities of exercising, and so strengthening, the graces of Christian living. Happy are they who are ever on the alert to manifest each grace, according to the successive demands of the varied experiences of daily life. If we were always on the lookout for opportunities of manifesting the special qualities of Christ's character that are called for by the trials and worries and difficulties of common experience, we should find that they were the twenty thousand chariots of God, waiting to carry us up to heights that could never otherwise be trodden by our feet.

BUT GOD ALWAYS PREPARES US FIRST

He "will with the temptation also make a way to escape, that ye may be able to bear it" (1 Cor. 10:13). Trials are therefore God's vote of confidence in us. Many seemingly insignificant events are sent to test us before a greater trial is permitted to break on our heads. We are sent to climb the lower peaks before we are urged to the loftiest summits with their virgin snows. We are made to run with footmen before contending with horses, and we are taught to wade in the shallows before venturing into the swell of the ocean waves. So it is written: "And it came to pass *after these things*, that God did tempt Abraham."

GOD OFTEN PREPARES US BY A NEW REVELATION OF HIMSELF

I notice that at the close of the preceding chapter, we are told that "Abraham...called there on the name of the LORD, the everlasting God" (Gen. 21:33). This is the first time that we learn that he had looked on God in this light. Abraham had known Him as God the Almighty (Gen. 17:1), but not as God the Everlasting. The unchangeableness, the eternity, the independence of change and time and tense that mark the Being of Jehovah—all these broke suddenly on his soul in a fresh and vivid manner. Anyone who can remember seeing the sea for the first time can never forget the first impression of its grandeur and endless, mirrorlike expanse. And the soul of the patriarch was thrilled with the lofty train of high and holy thought as he used that name in prayer beside the well and beneath the spreading shade of the tree he had planted. And with him, as so often with us, the new name was to enable him to better withstand the shock of coming sorrow.

THE TRIAL CAME VERY SUDDENLY

As we have seen, life was flowing smoothly with the patriarch—courted by Abimelech, secure of his wells, gladdened with the presence of Isaac and the everlasting God his Friend. "Ah, happy man!" we might well have exclaimed. "You have entered the glory land. Your sun shall no more go down nor your moon withdraw itself. Before you lie the sunlit years in an unbroken chain of blessing." But this was not to be. And just at that moment, like a bolt out of a clear sky, there burst upon him the severest trial of his life. It is not often that the express trains of heaven are announced by a warning bell or falling signal. They dash suddenly into the station of the soul. It is ours to be ever on the alert, for at such an hour and in such a guise as we think not, the Son of Man comes.

THE TRIAL TOUCHED ABRAHAM IN HIS TENDEREST POINT

It concerned his Isaac. Nothing else in the circumference of his life could have been such a test as anything connected with the heir of promise, the child of his old age, the laughter of his life. *His love was tested.* For his love of God, Abraham had done much. But at whatever cost, he had ever put God first, glad to sacrifice all, for very love of Him. For this he had torn himself from Charran. For this he had been willing to become a homeless wanderer, content if at the last he became a resident of God's home. For this he had renounced the hopes he had built on Ishmael, driving him, as a scapegoat, into the wilderness to return no more. But perhaps, if Abraham had been asked whether he felt that he loved God most of all, he would not have dared to say that he did. We can never gauge our love by feeling. The only true test of love is in how much we are prepared to do for the one to whom we profess it. "He that hath my commandments, and keepeth them, he it is that loveth me" (John 14:21). But God knew how true and strong His child's love was and that Abraham loved Him best. So He put him to a supreme test, that all men might henceforth know that a mortal man could love God so much as to put Him first, though his dearest lay in the opposite scale of the balance of the heart. Wouldn't you like to love God like this? Then tell Him you are willing to pay the cost if only He will create that love within you. And remember: though at first He may ask you to give up your Isaac to Him, it is only that you may take up your true position and demonstrate to the world your choice, for He will give your beloved back again from the altar on which you have lain him. "Take now thy son, thine only son Isaac, whom thou lovest,…and offer him there for a burnt offering" (Gen. 22:2).

It Was also a Great Test of His Faith

Isaac was the child of promise. "In Isaac shall thy seed be called" (Gen. 21:12). With reiterated emphasis this lad had been indicated as the one essential link between the aged pair and the vast posterity that was promised them. And now the father was asked to sacrifice Isaac's life. It was a tremendous test to his faith. How could God keep His word and let Isaac die? It was utterly inexplicable to human thought. If Isaac had been old enough to have a son who could perpetuate the seed to future generations, some of the difficulty would have been removed. But how could the childless Isaac die and still the promise stand of a posterity through him, innumerable as stars and sand? One thought, however, as the epistle to the Hebrews tells us, filled the old man's mind: "GOD IS ABLE." "Accounting that God was able to raise him up, even from the dead" (Heb. 11:19). He felt sure that somehow God would keep His word. It was not for Abraham to reason how, but simply to obey. He had already seen divine power giving life where all was as good as dead;

why should He not do it again? In any case, he must go straight on, doing as he was told and calculating on the unexhausted stores in the secret hand of God. Oh, for faith like this! Simply to believe what God says, assured that God will do just what He has promised, looking without alarm from circumstances that threaten to make the fulfillment impossible to the bare word of God's unswerving truthfulness. Surely this habit is not so impossible to attain. Why, then, should we not begin to practice it, stepping from stone to stone until we are far out from the shore of human resources, leaning on the unseen but felt arm of Omnipotence?

IT WAS A TEST OF ABRAHAM'S OBEDIENCE

It was in the visions of the night that the word of the Lord must have come to him, and early the next morning the patriarch was on his way. The night before, as he lay down, he had not the slightest idea of the mission on which he would be started when the early beams of dawn had broken up the short eastern night. But he acted immediately. We would have excused him if he had postponed his duty, procrastinating and lingering as long as possible. That, however, was not the habit of this heroic soul that had well acquired the habit of instant obedience, one of the most priceless acquisitions for any soul ambitious of saintliness. "And Abraham rose up early in the morning" (Gen. 22:3). No other hand was permitted to help or interfere with the promptness of his action. He "saddled his ass,...and clave the wood for the burnt offering, and rose up, and went unto the place of which God had told him." This promptness was his safeguard. While the herdsmen were beginning to stir and the long lines of cattle were being driven forth to their several grazing grounds, the old man was on his way. I do not think he confided his secret to a single soul, not even to Sarah. Why should he? The lad and he would enter that camp again when the short but awful journey was over. "I and the lad will go yonder and worship, and come again to you" (Gen. 22:5).

THIS TEST DID NOT OUTRAGE ABRAHAM'S SOUL

First of all, Abraham was too familiar with God's voice to mistake it. Too often had he listened to it to make a mistake in this solemn crisis. And he was sure that God had some way of deliverance that, though he might not be able to forecast it, would secure the sparing of Isaac's life. Besides, Abraham lived at a time when such sacrifices as that to which he was called were very common. He had never been taught decisively that they were abhorrent to the mind of his Almighty Friend. We must, in reading Scripture, remember that at first all God's servants were more or less affected by the religious notions that were current in their age. And we must not imagine that in all respects those early saints were divested of the misconceptions that resulted from the twilight revelation in which they lived but have since become dispersed before the meridian light of the gospel. One of the first principles of that old Canaaaitish religion demanded that men should give their firstborn for their transgression, the fruit of their body for the sin of their soul. On the altars of Moab and Phoenicia and Carthage, nay, even in the history of Israel itself—this almost irrepressible expression of human horror at sin and the desire to propitiate God found terrible expression. Not that fathers were less tender than now, but because they had a keener sense of the terror of unforgiven sin, they cowered before gods whom they knew not and to whom they imputed a thirst for blood and suffering. They counted no cost too great to appease the awful demands that ignorance and superstition and a consciousness of sin made upon them.

Perhaps Abraham had recently witnessed these rites, and as he did so, perhaps he had thought of Isaac and wondered whether he could do the same with his son, marveling why such a sacrifice had never been demanded at his hands. And it did not, therefore, startle him when God said, "Take now thy son, and offer him up." He was to learn that while God demanded as much love as ever the heathen gave their cruel and imaginary deities, yet heaven would not permit human sacrifices. A Greater Sacrifice was to be made to put away sin. Abraham's obedience was therefore allowed to go up to a certain point and was then peremptorily stopped—that in all future time men might know that God would not demand or permit or accept human blood at their hands, much less the blood of a bright and noble lad. In such things He could have no delight.

Let us ask ourselves whether we are of this same mind—holding our treasures with a loose hand, loving God most of all, prepared to obey Him at all costs, slaying our brightest hopes if God bid it—because we are so sure that He will not fail or deceive us. If so, may God give us this mind and keep us in it for His glory and for the maturing of our own faith.

What those three days of quiet traveling must have been to Abraham we can never know. It is always so much easier to act immediately than to wait through long days, and even years. But it is in this process of waiting upon God that souls are drawn out to a strength of purpose and nobility of daring that become their sacred inheritance for all time. And yet, despite the patriarch's preoccupation with his own special sorrow, the necessity was laid upon him to hide it under an appearance of resignation, so that neither his son nor his servants might guess the agony that was gnawing at his heart.

At last, on the third day, Abraham saw from afar the goal of his journey. God had informed him that He would tell him which of the mountains was the appointed spot of the sacrifice. As they arrived, probably some sudden conviction seized upon his soul that a specific summit that reared itself in the blue distance was to be the scene of that supreme act in which he should prove that to his soul God was chiefest and best. Tradition, which seems well authenticated, has always associated that mountain "in the land of Moriah" (Gen. 22:2) with the place on which stood the threshing floor of Araunah the Jebusite and the site of Solomon's temple in later years. There is a wonderful appropriateness in the fact that this great act of obedience took place on the very spot where great sacrifices of victims and rivers of blood were to point to that supreme Sacrifice that this prefigured.

As soon as the mountain had loomed into view, Abraham said to his young men: "Abide ye here with the ass; and I and the lad will go yonder and worship, and come again to you" (Gen. 22:5). What a significant expression is that word *worship!* It reflects the mood of the patriarch's mind. He was preoccupied with that Being, at whose command he had gone forth on this sorrowful errand. He looked upon his God, at the moment when He was asking so great a gift, as only deserving adoration and worship. The loftiest sentiment that can fill the heart of man swayed his whole nature, and it seemed to him as if his costliest and dearest treasure was not too great to give to that great and glorious God who was the one object of his life.

It is of the utmost importance that we should emphasize the words of *assured confidence* that Abraham addressed to his young men before he left them. "I and the lad will go yonder and worship, and come again to you." This was something more than unconscious prophecy: it was the assurance of an unwavering faith that somehow or other God would intervene to spare his son or, at least if necessary, to raise him from the dead. In any case, Abraham was sure that Isaac and he would before long come again. It is this that so largely removes the difficulties that might otherwise obscure this act, and it remains to all time a most striking proof of the tenacity with which faith can cling to the promises of God. When you have received a promise, cling to it as a sailor to a spar in the midst of the boiling waters. God is bound to be as good as His word. And even though He asks you to do the one thing that might seem to make deliverance impossible, yet if you dare to do it, you will find not only that you shall obtain the promise but also that you shall receive some crowning and unexpected mark of His love.

THE INFLUENCE OF ABRAHAM'S BEHAVIOR ON HIS SON

Isaac caught his father's spirit. We do not know how old he was. He was at least old enough to sustain the toil of a long march on foot and strong enough to carry uphill the wood that had been laid upon his shoulders by his father. But he gladly bent his youthful strength under the weight of the wood, just as through the *Via Dolorosa* One greater than he carried His cross. Probably this was not the first time that Abraham and Isaac had gone on such an errand, but it is beautiful to see the evident interest the lad took in the proceedings as they went, "both of them together."

At all previous sacrifices, Abraham had taken with him a lamb, but on this occasion, Isaac's wondering attention was drawn to the omission of that constant accessory to their acts of sacrifice. With a simplicity that must have touched Abraham to the heart, he said, "My father,...Behold the fire and the wood: but where is the lamb for a burnt offering?" (Gen. 22:7). What a stab this must have been to that troubled heart that dared not even reveal the secret beneath which it bowed and which eagerly caught at a device to enable it to postpone the answer. Thus with a gleam of prophetic insight, mingled with unwavering faith in Him for whose sake he was suffering, the father answered, "My son, God will provide himself a lamb for a burnt offering" (Gen. 22:8). So they went both of them together.

Do We Wonder at Abraham's Hiding the Facts?

We all have our treasures whom we fondly love. We shudder at the remotest thought of losing them. With breaking hearts we watch the color fade from the cheek of a darling child or mark the slow progress of disease in some beloved soul, but Abraham must submit to a keener test than these. Our dear ones depart in spite of all we do to keep them, but in Abraham's case there was the added anguish that he was to inflict the blow. The last thought that Isaac would have of his father would be holding the uplifted knife, and even though the lad might be restored to him, would it not be a revelation to the young heart to discover that it was possible for his father to do to him an act of violence like that?

Finally the Discovery Could No Longer Be Withheld

"And they came to the place which God had told him of; and Abraham built an altar there, and laid the wood in order" (Gen. 22:9). Can you not see the old man slowly gathering the stones, bringing them from the farthest distance possible, placing them with a reverent and judicious precision, and binding the wood with as much deliberation as possible? But at last everything is complete, and he turns to break the fatal secret to the young lad who had stood wonderingly by. Inspiration draws a veil over that last tender scene—the father's announcement of his mission, the broken sobs, the kisses, wet with tears, the instant submission of the son who was old enough and strong enough to rebel if he had wanted. Then came the binding of the tender body that needed no compulsion because the young heart had learned the secret of obedience and resignation. Finally, Abraham lifted him to lie upon the altar and wood. Here was a spectacle that must have arrested the attention of heaven. Here was a proof of how much mortal man will do for the love of God. Here was an evidence of childlike faith that must have thrilled the heart of the Eternal God and moved Him in the very depths of His being. Do you and I love God like this? Is He more to us than our nearest and dearest? Suppose they stood on this side, and He on that side: would we go with Him, though it cost us the loss of all? You think you would. Aye, it is a great thing to say. The

167

air upon this height is too rare to breathe with comfort. The one explanation of it is to be found in the words of our Lord: "He that loveth father or mother more than me is not worthy of me: and he that loveth son or daughter more than me is not worthy of me" (Matt. 10:37).

The blade was raised high, flashing in the rays of the morning sun, but it was not permitted to fall. With the temptation, God also made a way of escape. "And the angel of the LORD called unto him out of heaven, and said, Abraham" (Gen. 22:11). With what eagerness would his soul seize at anything that offered the chance of respite or of pause! And he said, his uplifted hand returning gladly to his side, "Here am I!" Would that we could more constantly live in the spirit of that response, so that God might always know where to find us and so that we might be always ready to fulfill His will. Then followed words that spoke release and deliverance: "Lay not thine hand upon the lad, neither do thou any thing unto him: for now I know that thou fearest God, seeing thou hast not withheld thy son, thine only son from me" (Gen. 22:12).

When we have given our best and costliest to God, passing our gifts through the fire, surrendering them to His will, He will give them back to us as gold refined—multiplied, as Job's belongings were. But it is also quite likely that He will not do so until we have almost lost all heart and hope. "Abraham called the name of that place, Jehovah-jireh" (Gen. 22:14), meaning that "the Lord will provide." And so it passed into a proverb, and men said one to another, "In the mount of the LORD it shall be seen" (Gen. 22:14). It is a true word. Deliverance is not seen till we come to the mount of sacrifice. God does not provide deliverance until we have reached the point of our extremest need. It is when our Isaac is on the altar and the knife is about to descend upon him that God's angel intervenes to deliver.

Nearby the altar was a thicket, and as Abraham lifted up his eyes and looked around, he beheld a ram caught there by its horns. Nothing could be more opportune. Abraham had wanted to show his gratitude and the fullness of his heart's devotion, and he gladly went and took the ram and offered him up for a burnt offering instead of his son. Here, surely, is the great doctrine of substitution, and we are taught how life can be preserved only at the cost of life given. All through this marvelous story there is an evident setting forth of the mysteries of Calvary.

Abraham's act enables us to more clearly understand the sacrifice that God made to save us. The gentle submission of Isaac as he was laid upon the altar with his throat bare to the knife gives us a better insight into Christ's obedience to death. Isaac's restoration to life, as from the dead, and after having been three days dead in his father's purpose, suggests the resurrection from Joseph's tomb. Yet the reality surpasses the shadow. Isaac suffers with a clear apprehension of his father's presence. Christ, deprived of the consciousness of His Father's love, complains of His forsakenness. All was done that love could do to alleviate Isaac's anguish, but Christ suffered the rudeness of coarse soldiery and the upbraidings of the Pharisees and scribes. Isaac was spared death, but Christ drank the bitter cup to its dregs.

Before they left the mountain brow, the angel of Jehovah once more addressed the patriarch. God had often promised, but now for the first time He swore; and since He could swear by no greater, He swore by Himself and said: "By myself have I sworn, saith the LORD, for because thou hast done this thing, and hast not withheld thy son, thine only son; that in blessing I will bless thee, and in multiplying I will multiply thy seed as the stars of heaven, and as the sand which is upon the sea shore; and thy seed shall possess the gate of his enemies; And in thy seed shall all the nations of the earth be blessed; because thou hast obeyed my voice" (Gen. 22:16–18).

Think not, O soul of man, that this is a unique and solitary experience. It is simply an example and pattern of God's dealings with all souls who are prepared to obey Him at whatever cost. After you have patiently endured, you shall receive the promise. The moment of supreme sacrifice shall be the moment of supreme and rapturous blessing. God's river, which is full of water, shall burst its banks and pour upon you a tide of wealth and grace. There is nothing, indeed, that God will not do for a man who dares to step out upon what seems to be the mist, though as he puts down his foot he finds it rock beneath him.

ALL WHO BELIEVE ARE THE CHILDREN OF ABRAHAM

We then, Gentiles though we are, divided from Abraham by the lapse of centuries, may inherit the blessing that he won, and the more so as we follow closely in his steps. That blessing is for us if we will claim it. That multiplication of seed may be realized in our fruitfulness of service. That victory over all enemies may give us victory in all the times of our temptation, and that blessing for all the nations of the earth may be verified again as we go forth into all the world telling the story of a Savior's death.

From that eminence, Abraham looked across the vale of centuries and saw the day of Christ. "He saw it, and was glad" (John 8:56). With a new light in his heart, with a new composure on his face, talking much with Isaac of the vision that had broken upon his noble soul, Abraham returned to his young men. "And they rose up and went together to Beersheba; and Abraham dwelt at Beersheba." But the halo of the vision lit up the ordinary places of his life, as it shall do for us when from the mounts of sacrifice we turn back to the lowlands of daily duty.

22

Machpelah, and its First Tenant

Give me a possession of a buryingplace with you,
that I may bury my dead out of my sight....
And after this, Abraham buried Sarah his wife
in the cave of the field of Machpelah before Mamre.

Genesis 23:4, 19

When Abraham descended the slopes of Mount Moriah, hand in hand with Isaac, fifty years of his long life still lay before him. Of those fifty years, twenty-five passed away before the event recorded in this chapter. What happened in those serene and untroubled years that lie between these two chapters as a valley between two ridges of hills, we do not know. In all likelihood, one year was as much as possible like another. Few events broke their monotony. The river of Abraham's life had passed the rapids and narrows of its earlier course and now broadened into reaches of still water, over which its current glided with an almost imperceptible movement.

The changes that mark the progress of our years are unknown beneath those glorious skies that rain perpetual summer on the earth, and the uniformity of the climate is symbolic of the uniformity of the simple patriarchal life. The tending of vast flocks and herds, the perpetual recurrence of birth, marriage, and death among the vast household of slaves, the occasional interchange of hospitality with neighboring clans, special days for sacrifice and worship— these would be the most exciting episodes of that serene and calm existence that is separated as far as possible from our feverish, broken lives. And yet, is there so very much that we can pride ourselves in when we compare our days with those? True, there was not the technology of today that has sped up our world and gives us a constant interchange of news. But perhaps life may more fully attain its ideal and fulfill its purpose when its moments and hours are not dissipated by the constant intrusion of petty details, like those that make up the fabric of most of our existence.

Perhaps we can never realize how much the members of such a household as Abraham's would be to one another. Through long, unbroken periods they lived together, finding all their society in one another. The course of pastoral life left ample leisure for close personal relationships. It was inevitable that human lives spent under such circumstances should grow together, even as trees in a dense wood become so entangled and entwined that no human ingenuity can disentangle one from another. Thus, it must have happened that the loss through death of one loved and familiar face would leave a blank never to be filled and scarcely ever to be forgotten. We need not wonder, therefore, that so much stress is laid upon the death of Sarah, the chief event of those fifty years of Abraham's life. Nor need we regret that such extensive details are given of her death and burial, since they enable us to get a glimpse of the patriarch and see whether he has changed at all during the quarter of a century that has passed over him.

WE ARE FIRST ARRESTED BY ABRAHAM'S TEARS

"And Sarah died in Kirjath-arba; the same is Hebron in the land of Canaan" (Gen. 23:2). Abraham seems to have been away from home, perhaps at Beersheba, when she breathed her last, but he came at once "to mourn for Sarah, and to weep for her." This is the first time we read of Abraham weeping. We do not read that he wept when he crossed the Euphrates, having left home and kindred forever. There is no record of his tears when tidings came to him that

172

his nephew Lot was carried into captivity. He does not seem to have covered his pathway to Mount Moriah with the tears of his heart. But now that Sarah is lying dead before him, the fountains of his grief are broken up.

What made the difference? Ah, there is all the difference between *doing* God's will and *suffering* it! So long as we have something to do for God—whether it is a toilsome march or a battle or a sacrifice—we can keep back our tears and bear up with fortitude. The multiplicity of our engagements turns away our attention from our griefs. But when all is over, when there is nothing more to do, when we are left with the silent dead, requiring nothing more at our hands, when the last office is performed, the last flower arranged, the last touch given—then the tears come.

It is not surprising that Abraham wept. Sarah had been the partner of his life for seventy or eighty years. She was the only link to the home of his childhood. She alone could sympathize with him when he talked of Terah and Nahor, or of Haran and Ur of the Chaldees. She alone was left of all who thirty years before had shared the hardships of his pilgrimage. As he knelt by her side, what a tide of memories must have rushed over him of their common plans and hopes and fears and joys! He remembered her as the bright young wife, as the fellow pilgrim, as the childless persecutor of Hagar, as the prisoner of Pharaoh and Abimelech, as the loving mother of Isaac, and every memory would bring a fresh rush of tears.

There are some who chide tears as unmanly, unsubmissive, un-Christian. They would comfort us with chill and pious stoicism, bidding us meet the most distressing passages of our history with rigid and tearless countenance. With such the spirit of the gospel and of the Bible has little sympathy. We have no sympathy with a morbid sentimentality, but we may well question whether the man who cannot weep can really love. Sorrow is love widowed and bereaved, and where that is present, its most natural expression is in tears. Religion comes not to make us unnatural and inhuman but to purify and ennoble all those natural emotions with which our manifold nature is endowed. Jesus wept. Peter wept. The Ephesian converts wept on the neck of the apostle Paul, whose face they thought they were never to see again. Christ stands by each mourner, saying, "Weep, my child; weep, for I have wept."

Tears relieve the burning brain, as a shower the electric clouds. Tears discharge the insupportable agony of the heart, as an overflow lessens the pressure of the flood against the dam. Tears are the material out of which heaven weaves its brightest rainbows. Tears are transmuted into the jewels of better life, as the wounds in the oyster turn to pearls. Happy, however, is that man who, when he weeps for his departed, has not to reproach himself with bitter words. We cannot always understand what makes people weep when we stand with them on the loose earth beside the open grave. In many cases, their sorrow is due to pure affection; in some cases, however, there is an additional saltiness in their tears because of unspoken regret: "I wish that I had not acted so, that I could recall those words, that I had had another opportunity of expressing the love I really felt but hid, that I had taken more pains to curb myself, to be gentle, loving, endearing, and endeared. Oh, for one hour of explanation and confession and forgiveness!" Let us see to it that we may never have to drink such bitter ingredients in the cup of our bereavement. Let us not fail to give expression to those nobler feelings that often strive within our breasts but we too often repress.

And if some should read these words whose tears are the more bitter because they themselves are unsubmissive, let them remember that where they cannot feel resigned, they must will to be resigned, putting their will on God's side in this matter. Let them ask God to take it and fashion it according to His own, remembering that our only province is with the will. This is all God asks, and if this is right with Him, He will subdue every other thought and bring the whole being into a state of glad acquiescence. "I delight to do thy will, O my God" (Ps. 40:8). "Though he slay me, yet will I trust in him!" (Job 13:15).

NOTICE ABRAHAM'S CONFESSION

"And Abraham stood up from before his dead, and spake unto the sons of Heth, saying, I am a stranger and a sojourner with you: give me a possession of a burying place with you" (Gen. 23:3–4). See how sorrow reveals the heart. When all is going well, we wrap up our secrets, but when sorrow rends the veil, the *arcana* of the inner temple are laid bare! To look at Abraham as the great and wealthy patriarch, the emir, the chieftain of a mighty clan, we cannot guess his secret thoughts. He has been in the land for sixty-two years, and surely by this time he must have lost his first feelings of loneliness. He is probably as settled and naturalized as any of the princes round. So you might think, until he is widowed of his beloved Sarah! Then, amidst his grief, you hear the real man speaking his most secret thought: "I am a stranger and a sojourner with you."

These are very remarkable words, and they were never forgotten by his children. Speaking of the land of promise, God said to the people through Moses, "The land shall not be sold for ever: for the land is mine; for ye are strangers and sojourners with me" (Lev. 25:23). When David and his people made splendid preparations to build the temple, as their spokesman he said, "But who am I, and what is my people, that we should be able to offer so willingly after this sort? for all things come of thee, and of thine own have we given thee. For we are strangers before thee, and sojourners, as were all our fathers: our days on the earth are as a shadow, and there is none abiding" (1 Chron. 29:14–15). And, further, in one of his matchless psalms, David pleads, "Hear my prayer, O LORD, and give ear unto my cry; hold not thy peace at my tears: for I am a stranger with thee, and a sojourner, as all my fathers were" (Ps. 39:12). So deeply had those words of Abraham sunk into the national mind that the writer of Hebrews inscribes them over the cemetery where the great and the good of the Jewish nation lie entombed: "These all died in faith, not having received the promises, but having seen them afar off, and were persuaded of them, and embraced them, and confessed that they were strangers and pilgrims on the earth" (Heb. 11:13).

We may ask what it was that maintained this spirit in Abraham for so many years. There is but one answer: "For they that say such things declare plainly that they seek a country" (Heb. 11:14). That country is never looked upon by the sun or watered by the rivers of the earth or refreshed by the generous dews. It is the better country, even the heavenly one, the city that has foundations, whose builder and maker is God, the land that needs neither sun nor moon because the Lord God and the Lamb are the light thereof. Uprooted from the land of his birth, the patriarch could never take root again in any earthly country. His spirit was always on the alert, eagerly reaching out toward the city of God, the home where only such royal souls as his can meet their peers and find their rest. He refused to be content with anything short of this; and, therefore, God was not ashamed to be called his God, because He had prepared for him a city. How this elevation of soul shames some of us! In our better moments we say that our commonwealth is in heaven, but by our practical, daily life we deny it. We profess to look for a heavenly city, but we take good care to make for ourselves an assured position among the citizens of this world. We say we count all things dross, but the eagerness with which, rake in hand, we strive to heap together the treasures of earth is a startling commentary upon our words.

NOTICE ABRAHAM'S FAITH

Men customarily bury their dead beside their ancestors. The graves of past generations are the heritage of their posterity. By them, rather than by the habitations of the living, do tribes and races of men find their resting place. The American loves to visit the quiet English churchyard where his fathers lie. The Jew desires in old age to journey to Palestine, that dying he may be buried in soil consecrated by the remains of his race. And it may be that Abraham first thought of that far distant grave in Charran, where Terah and Haran lay buried. Should he take Sarah there? "No," he thought, "that country has no claim upon me now. The only land, indeed, on which I have a claim is this wherein I have been a stranger. In later days shall my children live here. Here the generations that bear my name shall spread themselves out as the sands on the seashore and as the stars in the midnight sky. It is proper, therefore, that I should place our grave, in which Sarah their mother and I their father shall lie, in the heart of the land—to be a nucleus around which our descendants shall gather in all coming time. Even though, as God has told me, four hundred years of suffering and furnace fire must pass before my children shall ultimately come here again, I will hold the land in pledge against their coming, sure that it shall be as God has said!"

It is very beautiful to mark the action of Abraham's faith in this matter and to see its outcome in his utter refusal to receive the land as a gift from any hand but that of God. When the chieftains to whom he made his appeal heard it, they instantly offered him the choice of their sepulcher, affirming that none of them would withhold his sepulcher from so mighty a prince. And afterward, when he sought their intercession with Ephron, the son of Zohar, for the obtaining of the cave of Machpelah that was at the end of his field, and Ephron proposed to give it him in the presence of the sons of his people, Abraham steadfastly refused. It was all his as the gift of God; it would be all his someday in fact; and in the meanwhile, he would purchase the temporary use of that which he could never accept as a gift from any but his Almighty Friend.

And so after many fair speeches in the dignified manner that still prevails among the people of the East, "the field, and the cave which was therein, and all the trees that were in the field,...were made sure unto Abraham for a possession in the presence of the children of Heth, before all that went in at the gate of his city" (Gen. 23:17–18). Their witness had the same binding effect in those ancient days as legal documents have in our own.

There Abraham buried Sarah; there Isaac and Ishmael buried Abraham; there they buried Isaac and Rebekah, his wife; there Jacob buried Leah; and there Joseph buried Jacob, his father, and there in all likelihood, untouched by the changes and storms that have swept around their quiet resting place, those remains are sleeping still, holding that land as a down payment and anticipating the time when on a larger and more prominent scale the promise of God to Abraham shall be accomplished.

Not yet has the divine promise been fully realized. The children of Abraham have possessed the land of promise for "but a little while" (Isa. 63:18). For long ages their adversaries have held sway there. But the days are hastening on when once more God will set His hand to gather His chosen people from all lands; and once again shall the hills and valleys and pasturelands of Palestine come into the possession of the seed of Abraham, the friend of God.

23

THE SOUL'S ANSWER TO THE DIVINE SUMMONS

I will go.
Genesis 24:58

*A*llow your mind to drift back for thirty-eight centuries. The soft light of an Oriental sunset falls gently on the fertile grazing grounds watered by the broad Euphrates. As its twilight gloom lights up all the landscapes dotted by flocks and huts and villages, it irradiates with a particular wealth of color the little town of Haran, founded one hundred years before by Terah, who, traveling northward from Ur, resolved to go no farther. The old man was deeply pained by the recent loss of his youngest son, and after him the infant settlement was named. And so in time, houses were built and surrounded by a wall in Oriental style. There Terah died, and it was from here that the caravan had started at the command of God across the terrible desert for the unknown land of promise. One branch of the family, however—that of Nahor—lived there still. His son Bethuel was the head; and in that family, at the time of which I speak, there was at least a mother, a brother named Laban, and a daughter in the first blush of girlish beauty, Rebekah.

It is Rebekah who occupies the central place in the pastoral scene before us. All her young life had been spent in that old town. She was the daughter of the sheik, yet she was not kept in that lethargic indolence that dares not soil the fingers with honest work—an idleness that is the curse of so many wealthy girls today. She could make savory meat and tend the flocks as her niece Rachel did in later years on that same spot and carry her pitcher gracefully poised upon her shoulder. She knew by name all the people who dwelt in that little town, and she had heard of those of her kindred who had gone beyond the great desert before her birth and of whom hardly a word had traveled back for so many years. She little guessed the greatness of the world and of her place in it. In her wildest dreams she never thought of doing more than living and dying within the narrow limits of her native place. Buoyant in step, modest in manner, pure in heart, amiable and generous, with a very lovely face, as the sacred story tells us—how little did she imagine that the wheel of God's providence was soon to take her out of her quiet home and whirl her into the mighty outer world that lay beyond the horizon of desert sand.

On a special evening a stranger halted at the well that was outside the little town. He had with him a stately caravan of ten camels, each richly laden, and all bearing traces of long travel. There the little company waited, as if not knowing what to do next. Its leader was probably the good Eliezer, the steward of Abraham's house, who had come there on a solemn commission from his master. Abraham was now advanced in years. Isaac his son was forty years of age, and the old man longed to see him suitably married. Though Abraham's faith never doubted that God would fulfill His promise of the seed, yet he was desirous of wrapping his aged arms around the second link between him and his posterity. He had therefore bound his trusty servant by a double oath: first, that he would take a wife for Isaac not from the daughters of the Canaanites around them but from his own kin at Haran; and second, that he would never be an accomplice to Isaac's return to the land that he had left. This solemn oath was lit up by the assurance of the old man that the Lord God of heaven, who took him from his father's house and the land of his kindred, would send His angel before him and would crown his mission with success.

Having arrived at the city well toward nightfall—"even the time that women go out to draw water" (Gen. 24:11)—the devout leader asked that God would send him "good speed," addressing the Almighty as the Lord God of his master Abraham and pleading that in prospering his way He would show kindness to his master. The simplicity and trustfulness of his prayer are very beautiful and are surely the result of the godliness that reigned in that vast encampment gathered around the wells of Beersheba, the result of Abraham's own close walk with God. There would be less fault to find with workers in the present day if they were treated as servants were once treated—as souls rather than hands—and if they were encouraged to imitate the character of those with whom they are in such close contact. Alas, that workers in Christian homes often find so little to attract them to the godliness that is professed but seldom practiced!

It is our privilege to talk with God about everything in life. The minutest things are not too small for Him who numbers the hairs of our heads. No day can we afford to spend without asking that He should send us good speed. Well would it be for us, as we stand by the well in the morning or in the evening, to commit our way to the Lord, trusting that He should bring it to pass. And if this is true of ordinary days, how much more of those days that decide destiny, that are the watershed of life, and in which plans are concluded that may affect every year for the rest of our life! Nor is it wrong for us to ask a sign from God, if by this we mean that He would permit the circumstances of our daily experience to indicate His will, confirming that which He has already impressed upon our own conscience. We have no right to ask for signs for the satisfaction of a morbid curiosity, but we are justified in asking for the concurrence of outward providence indicating the will of God. It was a holy and a happy inspiration that led the godly servant to ask that the young woman, who responded with courteous swiftness to his request for water, should be she whom God had appointed as a bride for his master's son. It happened to him as it will always happen to those who have learned to trust like little children, that "before he had done speaking," his answer was waiting by his side (Gen. 24:15).

We need not describe in detail all that followed: the gifts of jewelry; the reverent recognition of God's goodness in answering prayer as the man bowed his head and worshiped the Lord; the admiration of mother and brother at the splendid gifts; the breathless telling of the unexpected meeting; the offer of hospitality from Laban, whose notions of hospitality were quickened by his keen eye for gain as he saw the rich lading of the camels; the provision of straw and provender for the camels, of water for the feet of the weary drivers, of food for their leader, and the refusal to eat until his errand was unraveled and its purpose accomplished; the story, told in glowing words, of Abraham's greatness; the narrative of the wonderful way in which the speaker had been led and Rebekah indicated; the final request that her relatives would deal kindly and truly in the matter; and their unhesitating and swift consent in words that drew the old servant prostrate to the ground in holy ecstasy as he worshiped the Lord. "Behold," they said, "Rebekah is before thee, take her, and go, and let her be thy master's son's wife, as the LORD hath spoken" (Gen. 24:51).

Then from his treasures, he brought forth jewels of silver and gold and raiment with which to deck Rebekah's lovely form. Rebekah's mother and Laban also received precious things to their hearts' desire. "And they did eat and drink, he and the men that were with him, and tarried all night" (Gen. 24:54). In the early dawn, refusing all invitation to further waiting, Abraham's steward started back again, carrying with him Rebekah and her nurse. Through the fragrant morning *air*, the blessings of that little cluster of friendly hearts drifted to her ear. Seated on her camel and wrapped in a dream of girlish hope and wonder, Rebekah caught the last voice from her home. "And they blessed Rebekah, and said unto her, Thou art our sister, be thou the mother of thousands of millions, and let thy seed possess the gate of those which hate them" (Gen. 24:60).

We must thus pass over the details of this story that carries with it the stamp of inspiration and of truth. Suffice it to say that it has no superior in this book for its rich, soft, peaceful style. It is full of those touches of nature that make all men kinsmen and that move them everywhere alike. Let us now draw out two or three further lessons to illustrate by it the divine summons and the answer of the soul.

A LESSON TO THOSE WHO
CARRY THE SUMMONS OF GOD

Let us saturate our work with prayer. Like his master, the servant of Abraham would not take a single step without prayer. Not that he always spoke aloud. No one would have known that the old man prayed as he stood there by the well. Nor did he arbitrarily dictate to God, but he threw the whole responsibility of the matter upon Him who had ever shown Himself so true a Friend to his beloved master. He had a most difficult thing to do in which strong contingencies were running against him. Was it likely that a young girl would care to leave her home to cross the vast expanse of sand in company with him, a complete stranger, and to become the wife of one whom she had never seen? "Peradventure the woman will not follow me" (Gen. 24:39), and if she were willing, her relatives might not be. But he prayed, and prayed again, and God's good speed crowned his errand with complete success.

We, too, are sometimes sent on very unlikely errands. Humanly speaking, our mission seems likely to prove a failure, but those who trust in God have not the word *failure* in their vocabulary. Their hearts are centers from which the fragrance of silent prayer is ever exhaling into the presence of God. They succeed where they seem menaced with certain disappointment. Christian worker, never start on any mission for God, whether to an individual soul or to a congregation, without the prayer, "Send me good speed this day."

We must also wait upon God for direction. Abraham's steward asked that the chosen bride should be willing to draw water for his camels. This may seem insignificant to some, and yet it was a true test for a girl's nature. It showed a ready kindness of heart that was prepared to outrun the requirements of conventional politeness. It indicated a nature in which haughty pride had no place. Is it not a fact that in such small, unpretentious acts there is a sure index of character? Very often God's servants make great mistakes because they force themselves on people, not living in the will of God, not seeking the indication of His bidding, not waiting until He opens the door of circumstance into some new life. We do not always realize the solemn mystery that surrounds each human heart or the depths into which all spiritual consciousness may have receded or the thick crust of worldliness and carelessness that may have coated over the sensibilities of the being. God only understands all this, and we are wise to wait expectantly and trustfully for Him to open up the way of access into the citadel of the heart. We may be sure that in this God will not fail us, but that while we are speaking He will hear and answer.

Let us say much in praise of our Master. It is beautiful to notice how eloquent the old man is about his master. He does not say one word about himself or extol himself in any way, so absorbed was he in the story of his distant lord. Was not this also characteristic of the apostles, who preached not themselves but Christ Jesus the Lord and whose narratives are like crystal glass, letting only His glory through? Alas, that we so impose ourselves that men go away talking of us! Let us lose ourselves in our theme. And while we show the jewels of Christian character in our own behavior, let the theme of our message be: "The Lord Jehovah has greatly blessed our Master, Christ, and has given Him a name that is above every name and has raised Him to His own right hand in the heavenly places, far above all principality and power and every name that is named. He is worthy to receive power and riches and strength and honor and glory and blessing." And when success attends your words, be sure to give all the glory to Him from whom it has come.

THE SUMMONS ITSELF

The summons was a call to a simple girl to ally herself in marriage to one of the wealthiest and noblest of earth's aristocracy. It was sent not because of her worth or wealth or beauty but because it was so willed in the heart and counsel of Abraham. Such a call is sent to every soul that hears the gospel. In the heavenly azure depths lives the great Father God. He has one Son, His only begotten and well beloved. He has resolved to choose from among men those who as one Church shall constitute His bride forever. He sends this call to you not because you are worthy or wealthy or beautiful but because He has so willed it in the counsels of His own heart. He longs that you shall be willing to detach yourself from all that you hold dear. This is His message: "Hearken, O daughter, and consider, and incline thine ear; forget also thine own people, and thy father's house; So shall the king greatly desire thy beauty: for he is thy Lord; and worship thou him" (Ps. 45:10–11).

And if that call is obeyed, you shall lose your own name in His name; you shall be arrayed in His fair jewels; you shall share His wealth; you shall sit down with Him on His throne; all things shall be yours. Will you go with this Man? Will you leave all to be Christ's? Will you give your unseen Lover your heart to be His forever? Come and put yourself under the escort of the blessed Holy Spirit, who pleads the cause of Jesus, as did Abraham's servant that of Isaac, and let Him conduct you where Jesus is.

HOW TO DEAL WITH THIS SUMMONS

We must find room for it. "Come in, thou blessed of the LORD; wherefore standest thou without? for I have prepared the house, and room" (Gen. 24:31). "The Master saith, Where is the guest-chamber?" (Mark 14:14). There was no room for Christ in the inn, but we must make room for Him in the heart, or at least we must be willing that He should make room for Himself.

We must bear witness. "And the damsel ran, and told them of her mother's house" (Gen. 24:28). As soon as you have heard the call and received the jewels of promise that are the pledge of your inheritance, you must go home to your friends and tell them what great things the Lord has done for you.

We must not delay or confer with flesh and blood. People and circumstances would eagerly delay our starting on pilgrimage. This is Satan's method of breaking off the union forever. There must be no delay, but when the inquiry is put to us, "Wilt thou go with this man?" (Gen. 24:58), we must promptly and swiftly answer, "I will go."

The journey was long and toilsome, but all the way the heart of the young girl was sustained by the tidings told her by the faithful servant, who cheered the weary miles with stories of the home to which she was journeying and of the man with whom her life was to be united. She already loved him and eagerly desired to see him.

One evening the meeting came. Isaac had gone out to meditate in the evening, sadly lamenting the loss of his mother, eagerly anticipating the coming of his bride, and interweaving all with holy thought. And when he lifted up his eyes across the pastures, lo, the camels were coming, and the two young souls leapt to each other. It was a happy meeting that made Rebekah oblivious to all the trials and hardships of her journey and the loss of her friends. Was it not also a sign of the moment when the work of the Holy Spirit, our gracious Guide, will conclude in the presence of our Lord, the true

Bridegroom of saintly hearts, and we shall see His face, to be forever with Him, going no more out forever?

And after a while in that silent home, there was again the chatter of children's voices; and for several years the patriarch rejoiced in the presence of his grandchildren, to whom he would tell the history of the past, on which his aged soul loved to dwell. And of one story those lads would never tire; that which told how their father had once climbed the summit of Moriah, to be, as it were, raised from the dead.

24

GATHERED
TO HIS PEOPLE

And these are the days of the years
of Abraham's life which he lived,
a hundred threescore and fifteen years.
Then Abraham gave up the ghost,
and died in a good old age, an old man,
and full of years; and was gathered to his people.

Genesis 25:7–8

*N*o human life can compete with Abraham's for the widespread reverence that it has evoked among all races and throughout all time. The pious Jew looked forward to resting in the bosom of Father Abraham after death. The fact of descent from him was counted by thousands sufficient to secure them a passport into heaven. Apostles so opposite as Paul and James united in commending his example to the imitation of early Christians in an age that had seen the Lord Jesus Himself. The medieval Church canonized Abraham alone among Old Testament worthies, by no decree but by popular consent. Devout Muslims reverence his name as second only to that of their prophet. What was the secret of this widespread renown? It is not because he headed one of the greatest movements of the human family, or because he demonstrated manly and intellectual vigor, or because he possessed vast wealth. It was rather the remarkable nobility and grandeur of his spiritual life that has made him the object of veneration to all generations of mankind.

At the basis of his character was a mighty faith. "And he believed in the LORD" (Gen. 15:6). In that faith he left his native land and traveled to one that was promised but not clearly indicated. In that faith Abraham felt able to let Lot choose the best land for himself because he was sure that none could do better for himself than God was prepared to do for the one who trusted Him. In that faith he waited through long years, sure that God would give him the promised child. In that faith Abraham lived a nomad life, dwelling in tents, making no attempt to return to the settled country from which he had come out. Indeed, his soul was consumed with the passionate expectancy of the city of God. In that faith Abraham was prepared to offer Isaac, and in that faith he buried Sarah.

Do not suppose that his faith dwelt alone. On the contrary, it bore much fruit, for if we test him by those catalogues of the fruits of faith that are provided in the New Testament, we shall find that he manifested them all. Take, for instance, that chain of linked graces enumerated in 2 Peter 1:5–11. This is like a golden ladder that stretches across the chasm between heaven and earth and unites them.

To faith Abraham added virtue, or manly courage. What could have been more manly than the speed with which he armed his trained servants or than the heroism with which he, with a group of undisciplined shepherds, broke on the disciplined bands of Assyria, driving them before him as the chaff before the whirlwind and returning victorious down the long valley of the Jordan?

And to manly courage Abraham added knowledge. All his life he was a student in God's college of divinity. Year after year, fresh revelations of the character and attributes of God broke upon his soul. He grew in the knowledge of God and the divine nature, which at the first had been to him a complete unknown. Like a foreign country grows beneath one's elevated gaze, Abraham climbed through the years into closer fellowship with God, and from the summit looked down upon its lengths and breadths, its depths and heights, its oceans, mountain ranges, and plains.

And to knowledge Abraham added temperance, or self-control.

That he was master of himself is evident from the way in which he refused the offer of the King of Sodom and curbed his spirit amid the irritations caused by Lot's herdsmen. The strongest spirits are those that have the strongest hand upon themselves and are able, therefore, to do things that weaker men would fail in. There is no type of character more splendid than that of the man who is master of himself because he is the servant of God, and who can rule others well because he can rule himself well.

And to temperance, patience. Speaking of Abraham, the voice of New Testament inspiration affirms that he "patiently endured" (Heb. 6:15). No ordinary patience was that which waited through the long years, not murmuring or complaining, but prepared to abide God's time. Abraham did not require the earthly consolation and help of which the psalmist said, "Surely I have behaved and quieted myself, as a child that is weaned of his mother: my soul is even as a weaned child. Let Israel hope in the LORD from henceforth and for ever" (Ps. 131:2–3).

And to his patience he added godliness. One of his chief characteristics was his godliness—a constant sense of the presence of God in his life and a love and devotion to Him. Wherever Abraham pitched his tent, there his first care was to erect an altar. Shechem, Hebron, and Beersheba saw these emblems of his reverence and love. In every time of trouble he turned as naturally to God as a child to its father. There was such holy conversation between his spirit and that of God that the name by which he is now best known throughout the East is "The Friend"—a name that he holds *par excellence* and that has almost overshadowed the use of that name by which we know him best.

And to godliness Abraham added brotherly kindness. Some men who are devoted toward God are lacking in the tenderer qualities toward those most closely knit with them in family bonds. Not so with Abraham. He was full of affection. Beneath the calm exterior and the erect bearing of the mighty chieftain there beat a warm and affectionate heart. Listen to that passionate cry, "O that Ishmael might live before thee!" (Gen. 17:18). Remember God's own testimony to the affection he bore toward Isaac: "Thy son, thine only son Isaac, whom thou lovest" (Gen. 22:2). Abraham's nature therefore may be compared to those ranges of mighty hills whose summits rear themselves above the region of storms and hold converse with the skies, while their lower slopes are clothed with woods and meadows, where homesteads nestle and bright children string their necklaces of flowers with merry laughter.

And to brotherly kindness Abraham added charity, or love. In his dealings with men, he could afford to be generous, openhearted, openhanded; willing to pay the price demanded for Machpelah's cave without haggling or complaint; destitute of petty pride; affable, courteous, able to break out into sunny laughter; right with God, and therefore able to shed upon men the rays of a pleasant, restful noble heart.

All these things were in him and abounded, and they made him neither barren nor unfruitful; they made his calling and election sure; they prepared for him an *abundant entrance* into the everlasting kingdom of God our Savior. The thought that underlies Peter's expression in the Greek is richly significant. The words denote the welcome given by choral songs and joyous greetings to the conqueror who, laden with spoils, returned to his native city. And they indicate that for some favored souls, at least, there is waiting on the threshold of the other world a welcome so exuberant, so boisterous in its unutterable joy, so royally demonstrative, as to resemble that given in all times to those who have conferred great benefits or who have learned the art of stirring the loyal devotion of their fellows. If such an entrance could be accorded to anyone, certainly it would be to Abraham when, stooping beneath the weight of one hundred threescore and fifteen years, "he gave up the ghost, and died at a good old age, an old man, and full of years; and was gathered to his people."

"Abraham gave up the ghost." There was no reluctance in his death. He did not cling to life; he was glad to depart when the angel-messenger summoned him. With the readiness of glad consent, his spirit returned to God who gave it.

He was gathered to his people. This cannot refer to his body, for that did not sleep beside his ancestors, but slept side by side with Sarah's. Surely, then, it must refer to his spirit. The world's gray fathers knew little of the future, but they felt that there was somewhere a gathering place of their clan, where devout and holy souls passed from this world and went to rejoin its people—the people from which it had sprung, the people whose name it bore, and the people to which by its tastes and sympathies it was akin.

What a lovely synonym for death! To die is to rejoin our people, passing into a world where the great clan is gathering, welcoming with shouts each newcomer through the shadows. Where are your people? I trust they are God's people, and if so, those who bear your name, standing on the other shore, are more numerous than the handful gathered around you here. They constitute many whom you have never known but who know you, many whom you have loved and lost awhile, many who without you cannot be made perfect in their happiness. There they are, rank on rank, company on company, regiment on regiment, watching for your coming. Be sure you do not disappoint them! But remember, if your people are God's people, you cannot be gathered to them unless first in faith and love you are gathered to Him.

Little doubt had this noble man of the recognition of saintly spirits in the other world. It is a false conception that has filled some people's minds that the future will be lived with strange spirits, unknowing and unknown. Heaven is not a prison with tier on tier of cells. It is a *home!* And what is home without the recognition and love of fond hearts? So long as we read of David going to his child, of Paul anticipating the pleasure of meeting his converts again, and of the women and disciples being able to recognize the appearance and the love of the Savior amid the glory of the resurrection body, we may be prepared to believe, with the patriarch, that dying is a reunion with those to whom in the deepest sense we are related. Spiritual relationships are for all time and for eternity and will discover themselves through all worlds.

"And his sons Isaac and Ishmael buried him in the cave of Machpelah" (Gen. 25:9). There were great differences between these two. Ishmael, the child of his slave; Isaac, the child of the wedded wife. Ishmael, the offspring of expediency, Isaac, the son of promise. Ishmael was wild and masterful, strongly marked in his individuality, proud, independent, swift to take an insult, and swift to avenge it. Isaac was quiet and retiring, submissive and meek, willing to carry wood, to be kept in the dark, to be bound, to yield up his wells, and to let his wife govern his house. And yet all differences between the men were wiped out in that moment of supreme sorrow. Coming from his desert strongholds, surrounded by his wild and ruffian marauders, Ishmael united with the other son of their common father who had displaced him in his inheritance and was so great a contrast to himself. But all differences were smoothed out in that hour.

Many ancient chieftains may have been gathered by that ancient cave, joining in one last act of respect to the mighty prince who had dwelt among them for so long. Amid the wail of the women and the lament that even to this day tells of sorrow in eastern lands, Abraham was borne by a band of his trusted servants while a vast concourse of the camp stood wrapped in reverent silence around. The remains of the man who had dared to trust God at all costs and who with pilgrim steps had traversed so many weary miles were solemnly laid beside the dust of Sarah, his faithful wife. There, in all probability, they rest even to this day, and from here they will be raised at the coming of the King.

Out of materials that were by no means extraordinary, God raised up a character with whom He could hold fellowship as friend with friend, and the result was a life that has exerted a profound influence for all time. It would seem as if He can raise any crop He chooses when the soil of the heart and life is entirely surrendered to Him. Why would we not yield ourselves utterly to His divine hand, asking Him to fulfill in us the good pleasure of His goodness and the work of faith with power? Only let us trust Him fully and obey Him instantly and utterly; and as the years pass by, they shall witness results that will bring glory to God in the highest, while they fill us with ceaseless praise.